THE
STUDENT
ATHLETE'S
HANDBOOK

The Complete Guide
for Success

**PERRY BROMWELL and
HOWARD GENSLER**

Foreword by Steve Young of the San Francisco 49ers

John Wiley & Sons, Inc.

New York ▸ Chichester ▸ Weinheim ▸ Brisbane ▸ Singapore ▸ Toronto

Published by John Wiley & Sons, Inc.

This publication is designed to provide accurate and authoritative information in regard to the subject matter covered. It is sold with the understanding that the publisher is not engaged in rendering professional services. If legal, accounting, medical, psychological, or any other expert assistance is required, the services of a competent professional person should be sought.

Library of Congress Cataloging-in-Publication Data

Bromwell, Perry
    The student athlete's handbook : the complete guide for success /
Perry Bromwell and Howard Gensler ; foreword by Steve Young.
      p. cm.
    Includes index.
    ISBN 0-471-14975-6 (paper : alk. paper)
    1. College student orientation—United States—Handbooks, manuals,
etc. 2. College athletes—United States—Handbooks, manuals, etc.
3. College sports—United States—Handbooks, manuals, etc.
I. Gensler, Howard. II. Title.
LB2343.32.B74 1997
796.04'3—dc21   97-19049
                                                       CIP

Contents

Foreword

I am one of the lucky ones. When I was growing up in Connecticut, I loved to play sports—football, basketball, whatever my friends and I wanted to do. Sports was an outlet for youthful energy and a means to build friendships. Most of all, it was fun. Then, the idea that I could continue to be active in sports through college and, ultimately, become a professional was a dream.

I was able to attain that dream. I got the chance to be the starting quarterback for Brigham Young University's football team, where I could compete at the highest level. My team won all but one game my senior year, including a bowl game. Individually, I received many honors, including being named an All-American and finishing second in the Heisman Trophy voting. I even set an NCAA record for completion percentage. This success gave me the opportunity to play professional football, allowing me to extend my involvement in athletics to the pros.

As important a part of my life as football was during college, though, it was only one part of my life. I went to college to get an education, and I got a great one at BYU. I went to college to make friends, to form lifelong relationships, and to get more in touch with my community. I was able to accomplish these things, too. These are the rewards of college that last long after an athletic career is over.

This book is about making the right decisions. What are you trying to get out of college, and how are you going to get those things? Which college is right for you? What role is sports going to take in your collegiate life? How can you succeed, in sports and in life, wherever you go?

I chose BYU for many reasons. I was born in Salt Lake City, not far from the school. BYU and Utah are important to my family and my religious faith. I knew I would get a great education in a support-ive environment. I knew I could play football at the highest collegiate level; in fact, I played in one of the best systems for quarterbacks any-where in the country. For me, the decision to enroll at BYU was clearly the right choice.

By choosing the right college and by making some good deci-sions once I got there, I was fortunate enough to be able to extend my dream. The professional football life is challenging: there is a great deal of pressure, there have been some painful injuries, and there are frustrations when you're not playing as well as you'd like or as often as you'd like. But the rewards have been tremendous. I've had the opportunity to win Super Bowl rings, to gain financial security, to meet people, and to do things that probably wouldn't have been pos-sible without sports.

I've done my best to continue to make the right decisions. In the off-seasons, I attended BYU's law school and earned my law degree—my dad's a lawyer and, since I won't be able to play football forever, additional education can never hurt. I've dedicated my time and energies off the field to my charitable foundation, the Forever Young Foundation, and to speaking engagements and other events designed to improve the world that we all share.

If you're reading this book, you (or someone close to you) are probably interested in having athletics play a role in your life in col-lege and maybe beyond. If you are fortunate enough to have the opportunity, enjoy it. If you're gifted enough and lucky enough to continue on to a career in sports, perhaps as a professional or as an international competitor, count yourself among the truly blessed. Whatever your athletic ability and interest brings you, I hope you are able to enjoy all of the other benefits college can bring you, too. If you can do that, then you have succeeded.

—Steve Young,
Quarterback,
San Francisco 49ers

Acknowledgments

In addition to San Francisco 49ers quarterback Steve Young, who was not compensated for his participation in this project, and the athletes, coaches, agents, and others who graciously gave of their time in order to be interviewed for this book, the authors would like to thank: Leigh Steinberg, Jeff Moorad, Scott Parker, Reya Ingle, and Marina Costabile of Steinberg & Moorad; Stefani Wanikur of SKS Management; The Forever Young Foundation; Peter Roisman, Joel Bell, Debby Zealley, and Hillary Schubach of Advantage International; and Stefan Fatsis, David Grubman, Bryan Harris, John Langel, Milton Lewin, Liz McMillen, Jack Reale, Alan Schwarz, Penn Basketball coaches Fran Dunphy, Gil Jackson, Steve Donahue, and David Hooks and Michael V. Earle of the NCAA.

We would also like to thank Ed Knappman of New England Publishing Associates for his belief in this project, his work to make it happen, and his continued advice and support; and editor Judith N. McCarthy of John Wiley & Sons for her questions, patience, and good humor as deadline after deadline rolled by. Also thanks to John Wiley's Elaine O'Neal, Diane Aronson, and Benjamin Hamilton. All have worked to make this book infinitely better than it might have been.

Perry Bromwell would like to give spiritual thanks to the Almighty for strength and persistence. Supportive thanks to Mother V.B.J. and my loving family: Coryn, Crystal, DeLisa, Reneé, Devone, Vonda, Lyric, J.J., Joseph, and several others. Amicable thanks to many friends, associates, and those who contributed to this book. Thanks also to my coauthor, Howard Gensler.

Howard Gensler would like to thank his parents, Sally and Milton Gensler, for their continued love and support, and Perry Bromwell for coming up with the idea for this book oh, so many years ago.

High School

1 Why College?

● ● ● ●

As the world around us changes at an ever-faster rate and exciting technological advances in computers, medicine, and more send us hurtling into the next century, an education will become an even more important key to success. The jobs of the past, which could be had with just a high school diploma, are disappearing, and advanced degrees and areas of expertise are becoming the norm in the workforce.

For the high school student athlete, college is a logical and important step toward a career as a professional (doctor, lawyer, athlete) in any walk of life. A college degree opens doors, garners respect, and, to many, is still a symbol of status and achievement.

College, however, is more than an essential stepping-stone to a career outside of athletics. Unless you are a tennis phenom on the pro circuit at the age of 15 or a baseball prospect with a chance to sign a million-dollar deal out of high school (we'll get to that later), college is also the best avenue to advance your chances for a professional career inside of athletics. In basketball, football, track, soccer, golf, and more, the majority of professional athletes come from the collegiate ranks. Becoming a professional athlete is a long shot, to be sure, but college is a ticket to all sorts of economic opportunities.

Four years at college does even more than provide you with a means toward a job and economic security. As a bridge between your teenage years and adulthood, college comes at a time when your body and mind are developing at a dizzying rate, when your world is seen in terms of possibilities and not limitations and when you can set the groundwork to become all that you want to be.

As a high school student athlete, Dallas Cowboy running back **Herschel Walker** could have easily relied solely on his athletic ability to try to achieve his goals. Walker was big, strong, and could run like the wind—a world-class football player *and* a world-class sprinter. But Walker, who would later win the Heisman Trophy at the University of Georgia, knew that football could only take him so far. "Knowledge is everything," he says. "They can take away your athletic ability. They can take away so many things from you. But the one thing they can never take away from you is your mind. Knowledge is like a blessing. And if God gives you that blessing you want to mature with it."

That's where college comes in—to expand your mind and show you that there's a great big world out there beyond your neighborhood, mall, or street corner. And while you think that much of the information that will be forced upon you in high school and even more so in college—in mathematics, literature, history, and science—has little bearing on your future, you're probably wrong. Geometry might come in handy should you want to design something (from a bookcase to a house) in the future. The ability to appreciate literature (and art) will allow for peaceful contemplation and time away from the pressures of modern living and the competition of sports. In addition, the ability to read well will improve your vocabulary and your ability to communicate—a most important skill for anyone. An understanding of biology and human anatomy will give you important insight into how your body works (a good thing for an athlete) and possibly make you a more knowledgeable patient should you be injured at some point in your athletic career. A knowledge of history allows you to view world events and the development of your sport with a certain amount of perspective—and an interest in what has come before you frequently creates an interest in what lies ahead.

More important than all of that learning, however, is learning how to learn, because learning is a skill that needs to be practiced and nurtured more than any other skill. Knowledge is what drives us forward and allows us to improve. As Franklin D. Roosevelt said in 1932, "Knowledge—that is, education in its true sense—is our best protection against unreasoning prejudice and panic-making fear, whether engendered by special interest, illiberal minorities, or panic-stricken leaders."

Outfielder **Milt Thompson,** a 10-year major leaguer who attended Howard University, puts it a little differently. "It's important to get all the book knowledge you can," he says. "You can get knowledge on the streets, but there's certain book knowledge you can't get on the streets. That's why school is very important."

So it's a given that college will fill your head with new ideas. Here are some of the other "new" things college will offer you.

A New World

For many, college is the first chance to live in a completely new environment. It's the first chance to *really* experience a world beyond your neighborhood. If you choose to attend a school far away from home, everything might seem new to you: the environment, the terrain, the weather, the culture, and, of course, the people. But even attending a college close to home offers an entirely new perspective on the world. When you're on campus, it doesn't matter how near or far you are from home—it's still different.

Baltimore Oriole outfielder/designated hitter **Pete Incaviglia** was chosen in the 10th round of the Major League Baseball draft by the San Francisco Giants but passed up his signing bonus to move 1,000 miles to play baseball for Oklahoma University—where he would become the leading home run hitter in NCAA history. As he tells it: "I grew up in Monterey, California, and I went to Oklahoma and I didn't know one person in Oklahoma. I started to become an adult and learn responsibilities. I learned to do a lot of things that prepared me for where I am now."

New People

College gives you a chance to make new friends—from different neighborhoods and different parts of the country. Depending on the high school you come from and the college you choose to attend, it might offer you exposure to ethnic groups you've never met before or students from different economic classes than the ones you have known growing up. By putting you in closer proximity to groups you may have never had close contact with before, college frequently forces you to socialize with people beyond your previous comfort zone and thereby forces you to confront your fears and prejudices.

Many students from sheltered or nondiverse backgrounds find the cultural exchange that college often brings is as important as the exchange of ideas that takes place. Campus cultural organizations often help students learn more about their own culture and heritage—often for the first time.

As a student athlete, you're also likely to come into contact with important and influential alumni who can help you during your college years and—most important—after college. For a teenager, meeting a prominent alum can be a little terrifying—you don't want to make a fool of yourself—but networking is an important skill to learn and college is a great place to learn it.

New Responsibilities

Unless you're a commuter student living at home, college teaches you how to live on your own and forces you to be responsible for your own actions and your own time. For many teenagers, college will be the first chance to practice living as an adult: making decisions, solving problems, and handling diversity *and* adversity. Nobody, except a concerned coach, bugs you to do anything at college. You're responsible for getting up and getting places on time, keeping your room clean, budgeting your money, and balancing your work with your social activities. For some, all of this freedom can be daunting. There's a temptation to spend more money on clothes, music, et cetera in order to keep up with fashion, to party later and harder, to sleep less and eat worse, and continually to push off doing your schoolwork to a future time that never seems to be there when you need it. How to discipline yourself—figuring out what you have to do to motivate yourself to accept all these new responsibilities—is one of the most important things you can learn at college.

Says Herschel Walker: "One thing college does is bring out maturity because you're on your own. You don't have your parents there saying you've got to go to bed at this time, you need to do this, you need to do that. You've got to do it on your own. If your work is not done, you're going to get kicked out of school. The responsibility is put on you."

Another important step in this ongoing maturation process is learning to ask for help. You don't know everything and nobody expects you to know everything. If you feel yourself sinking under the weight of your schoolwork, your athletic work, a social crisis, or a health crisis, there are people to see for advice. Don't be ashamed to ask for help. And don't forget about your relatives and friends back home. One of your other important responsibilities is to let them know how you're doing and also see how they're doing with you away.

In college, you'll find that your responsibilities continue to evolve. Your sports role might change from that of a rookie learning to fit in to that of team leader, team spokesperson, or team captain. Whereas you might be asking all the questions during your freshman year, you might be asked for all the answers by your senior year. And if you become a prominent figure on campus, due either to your intelligence, your personality, or your prowess in athletics, you might find yourself responsible for answering questions about areas of collegiate life (race relations, for example) that you have little or no control over.

Since there is undeniably a suspicion about the classroom caliber of student athletes—especially at the schools with greater academic prestige—you may also find yourself responsible, albeit unfairly, for proving to your fellow students that you and your team members belong. Your work and your behavior will be watched—and analyzed—almost as much as your ability to play your sport (see chapter 9). You may find this especially true if you are a member of a minority, depending on where you choose to go to school. This double standard may place you under unreasonable pressure—it's hard enough to keep up with your practice schedule, your personal workouts, your social calendar, and your classroom work—but one of the ways student athletes, especially big-name student athletes, grow as people is to develop their ability to deal with this added pressure.

New Challenges

In addition to the all-important challenge of growing up that college provides, the move from high school provides the student athlete with challenges in sports and in the classroom. The classroom challenges may be especially tough since college work is often very different from high school work—there's more reading, more writing, and, most important, more analysis. You can't just try to memorize everything as if it were a playbook. Your college work might not always seem applicable to your everyday life, but that's an important part of the academic challenge—a good liberal arts college education will teach you the value of learning for the sake of learning and also the value of the theoretical model over the practical application.

If you are not academically challenged by your college courses, then the courses are too easy or you are being catered to because you are an athlete. Don't take the easy way out. Prove to those who put you down that you are more than just an athlete. You're a student, too. Passing a difficult course can be a huge confidence builder that will carry into your athletic career and your life.

Another challenge: Since a large number of high school students don't have the grades or the desire to continue their education after high school, there's a lot higher level of competition, in all areas, when you get to college; the unruly, lazy kids who who made you look so smart or so talented in high school have been weeded out. Many incoming freshmen are rudely awakened very shortly after they arrive on campus—they find they are no longer the smartest, the fastest, or the strongest. A high school valedictorian might suddenly find him/herself in the company of a dozen other valedictorians, especially at one of the better universities. And an all-city or all-state athlete might encounter a surprising number of athletes of similar caliber at the first practice. Dealing with your newfound status on the playing field and in the classroom is essential to making the adjustment from high school to college.

College gives you a chance to see where you stack up against students and athletes from other parts of the country. You may have been #1 in your class at a small rural high school or at a large urban high school, but how does your education stack up against the private, parochial, and boarding school kids you might encounter at college. Whereas you might have dominated your sport in high school, perhaps even at the conference or area level, in college you'll get a chance to see how you compare to other student athletes who've been recruited from distant areas to play with and against you. It's therefore essential to have a realistic sense of your level of ability (see chapter 2) so that you can try to put yourself in a situation that gives you the maximum opportunity to excel.

Herschel Walker says that one of the most important qualities you need to excel is patience. "At college, you've got to have patience," he says. "You've got to know your priorities. You've got to know what you have to do to control your life. Even though college is a lot of fun, sometimes you can't have a lot of fun. First things first. And the first thing is to get in your classwork. If you're in college on scholarship, your athletic ability is there. But what you want to do is develop your mental ability and that means being able to study."

New Places

For many student athletes, college provides the first opportunity to travel to other parts of the country and the world. For some, just getting to college will be a big trip. But at the Division I level, especially in the larger athletic conferences, you'll spend almost as much time on planes and buses during the season as you will in the classroom. Intersectional games, for instance, might mean a trip across the entire country. And if you or your team advances to an NCAA tournament, a bowl game, or the College World Series, that will mean even more traveling. This traveling can be fun and exciting, but it can also present huge problems for the student athlete who doesn't keep up with his or her schoolwork (see chapter 8). That student will fall behind in a hurry.

There are also ways that playing on a college team allows you to see the world even if your team plays all of its games within 50 miles of your campus. Collegiate all-star teams (in most sports) frequently travel overseas for exhibitions and clinics. Some individual college teams even make an occasional trip during the summer to Europe, Asia, or South America. And, of course, for the absolute best, there are always the Pan-Am Games, the world championships, the Olympics, and other international events.

• • • •

One last point: Having college as a goal will improve your high school experience. If you view high school as the end of your education, you are less likely to take the work seriously. If, however, your performance in high school—academically and athletically—has an impact on your future dreams, you may pay that much more attention and work that much harder. And if your dreams include a career as a professional athlete, you have virtually no chance without a high school diploma, and a significantly greater chance if you get the education, exposure, and environment in which to mature that college can provide.

College Options

NCAA: Division I

Taking it as a given that going to college, if you have the opportunity, is a good thing, it's important to understand your college options. Most people, when talking about college athletics, are talking about Division I, the 300+ large NCAA schools whose competition generates most of the media attention given to college sports and whose championship in basketball and New Year's bowl games in football score huge television ratings. Almost all of the schools in Division I offer sports scholarships—-the exceptions being the Ivy League and

Patriot League schools, the service academies, and Prairie View A&M. All of those schools, however, do offer financial aid.

If you think you're good enough to play big-time college athletics, you're probably thinking about playing at the Division I level, but keep your options open—Division I may not be the best fit for you.

NCAA: Division II

Although Division II schools can be large in size, their athletic ambitions, budgets, and facilities (stadiums, arenas, etc.) are below the standard necessary to compete at the Division I level. Some Division II schools, however, do participate in Division I in certain sports. There are more than 200 Division II schools and they do offer athletic scholarships, but not in the quantity of their Division I counterparts.

NCAA: Division III

There are approximately 350 schools playing at the Division III level, although, again, some may participate in Divisions I or II in certain sports. Generally, Division III schools *do not* provide athletic scholarships, although most do offer need-based and non-need-based financial aid. Some of the nation's most prestigious small colleges compete at the Division III level.

• • • •

Since NCAA rules are constantly changing, for the latest information about the NCAA and its member schools, contact:

National Collegiate Athletic Association
6201 College Boulevard
Overland Park, KS 66211–2422

Which NCAA Division Is Best for You?

Although Division I colleges and universities get the bulk of media attention and exposure, Division I is not always the best choice for every student athlete. For some, whose high school grades or test scores do not pan out, Division I will not be an option coming out of high school, but even if you have the grades (and think you have the game), if you're not planning on a career as a professional athlete you may want to at least consider some schools in Divisions II or III—especially if you're not receiving the recruiting interest you believe you deserve.

Think Division I is the only game in town? Think again. As basketball coach at Philadelphia's Simon Gratz High School, **Bill Ellerbee** has coached numerous players who've gone on to play college basketball and a few (including Portland Trail Blazers Rasheed Wallace and Aaron McKie) who've made it all the way to the NBA. Many of Ellerbee's players go on to play at the top Division I programs, but he says of his players that "one thing you've got to do is keep them rooted in reality. You have to make sure they're aware what's available to them in choosing a college. And sometimes they just don't know the opportunities that are there for them at the Division II and Division III levels. They look at it like if they don't go to a Division I school that it's like death."

Boston Celtics scout **Leo Papile**, a longtime Boston AAU basketball coach whose program has also sent players to the game's highest levels, agrees. "What too often happens," Papile says, "is that a kid will get some bad advice and think he can go to Boston College or Northeastern when he'd be much better off going to Bridgewater State or UMass-Boston, which is not bad. Let's face it, there's Division I, II, and III, and NAIA for a purpose. Not everyone can be at one of those three hundred Division I schools. You can still have a great college basketball experience."

As the director of the Penn Relays, the world's largest track and field meet, **Dave Johnson** has cause to interact with countless high school and college track athletes. He's a strong booster of Divisions II and III.

Johnson says that too often a high school student athlete opts for a Division I school where he faces four years as a benchwarmer, "whereas if that same athlete coming out of high school had gone to a D-II or D-III school, he might find that he's competing in his freshman year. That way he's able to maintain that athletic balance to his own life that was important to him in high school.

"Just because you're coming out of high school and you're making a change doesn't mean that you have to change everything. You should remember some of the things that kept you interested in everything that you were doing. Don't sacrifice it for the name of a big school. It's a very small number of kids who are able to go on to a D-I scholarship school. Far fewer make it at that level than the promise is there for."

In addition, Johnson says that programs at the Division II and III levels are more forgiving of faults and more able to allow an athlete to mature and improve at his/her own pace. "A high school coach might see a spark in a good athlete that makes him think he can make it in a D-I program," says Johnson, "but maybe he's only looking at the kid's work ethic or his size or his quickness. The problem is to make it at Division I you need the whole package or it doesn't work. You go to a D-III school and you might be able to get by with only two out of four or five of those qualities and have time to develop the others."

Lastly, Johnson says student athletes might be wise to skip the pressures of Division I if they enjoy playing their sport but are not consumed by it. If that's the case, "maybe D-I's not for you," he says. "Maybe you need to drop down a level where you can perform at a level that's acceptable to you without working at becoming any better. It's very difficult to gauge but the more insight you have into yourself the better off you are."

Alternatives to the NCAA

The three divisions administered by the NCAA, however, don't comprise all your options. There are other schools to consider if your grades and test scores are good and a few options if you haven't been able to make the grade.

Prep School

Prep schools serve a few purposes. Unlike many public schools struggling to survive with limited funding and decaying classrooms, prep schools frequently provide a safer academic haven with individualized education, college-oriented courses, and lots of tutors. If prep school is affordable or financial aid is available, many student athletes make the jump to prep school early to improve their chances of getting into the college of their choice.

For others, prep schools serve as a bridge between high school and college, either as a means to improve one's academic standing in order to gain academic acceptance at one's college of choice or as a means to improve one's athletic standing, by allowing one's body and skills to mature for an extra year without losing a year of collegiate eligibility.

If prep school holds some interest for you, you should speak with your coach or academic adviser. Many prep schools across the country have excellent reputations for preparing struggling students for the rigors of college, and, in this era of specialization, many prep schools have developed reputations for excelling in various sports, offering student athletes a chance to get accustomed to college-level work *and* college-level athletics.

Occasionally a college coach will talk to you about the prep school alternative. If you have interest in an Ivy League school or another elite academic institution, but your academics are, at best, borderline for acceptance, a coach might suggest you think about prep school and possibly even suggest a prep school where:

- there is some history of the prep school working as a feeder school to his/her university;
- he/she can keep an eye on you *and* know if your improvement is suddenly making you more attractive to other recruiters.

If you have your heart set on attending a Division I school and you're just not ready, taking a postgraduate year at a prep school may be an option worth considering.

Junior College

Another option to consider is junior college. You don't need a specific SAT score to be accepted into a junior college and sometimes you don't even need to have graduated from high school—as long as you complete one term of college work with a full course load and a GPA of at least 1.75.

A proponent of junior colleges is **Saudia Roundtree,** the Naismith Award–winning All-American guard from the University of

Georgia. Although Roundtree had performed well in her high school classes, she did not achieve the required SAT score to be eligible at Georgia, to whom she had committed, as a freshman. She wasn't sure what she was going to do after high school, but one thing was certain: she did not want to go to junior college.

"I would never even talk to any junior college coaches," she says. "And then [Kilgore College, Texas] Coach [Evelyn] Blalock just called me one day out of the blue and I don't know what made me talk to her—I honestly think it was God—because I wouldn't talk to anybody. But she called and she said 'just listen to what I have to say.' Other people had done that but I didn't really listen. But I listened to what she said, and she said 'I'm not making any promises that you'll start here' and that was the key because I don't want anybody promising me anything. I want to go out and work for everything that I get. So that just made me think that this lady is for real. So she told me to come out there and if I didn't like it I could leave. So I went out there and I liked her and liked the school—it was in an atmosphere that I knew I would get my work done and the people there just love basketball."

And the rest is college basketball history. Roundtree got her academics in order off the court and on the court helped lead the Kilgore Lady Rangers to the 1993 National Junior College title. In 1994 she was named national junior college player of the year. After that it was back to Georgia, finally as a student athlete, and honors as the 1996 SEC player of the year and the national player of the year. Last year, Roundtree signed a contract to endorse Reebok basketball shoes and also inked a professional deal with the Atlanta Glory in one of the two new women's pro basketball leagues.

"A lot of students who don't get their test scores coming out of high school get discouraged," she says, "because they're thinking that they're never going to get to Division I. They think they're not going to be successful. They're saying, 'I have to go to junior college and I'm not going to be successful.' But a junior college is to help you get your priorities in order, to help you to make yourself more academically aware as to what you need to do. That's what junior college did for me. That's the best thing that could have ever happened to me as

far as academics because I had to put my priorities in order in order
to go Division I.

"I had a dream to go to Division I but the only thing I could do
to go to Division I was to graduate from a junior college. And when
you have your priorities in order and you have goals, then you're going to achieve those goals if you really want them.

"Unfortunately, some people go to junior college and do the
same thing they probably did in high school—which is nothing. They
go and never make it to Division I."

The key, says Roundtree, no matter where you go, is to take responsibility for yourself. "Your coach and your family can only do so
much. It's the individual who has to go into the classroom and do the
work. There are people helping you—tutors if you need them—giving you the academic help that you need, but can't nobody go in and
take a test for you and can't nobody study for you. You've got to be
self-disciplined and have your priorities in order and do what you
need to do."

Junior colleges compete in baseball, basketball, bowling, cross
country, football, golf, ice hockey, lacrosse, soccer, swimming, tennis,
track and wrestling. For the latest information about junior colleges,
talk to your coach or adviser or contact:

National Junior College Athletic Association (NJCAA)
P.O. Box 7305
Colorado Springs, CO 80933–7305

NAIA

There are nearly 400 fully-accredited four-year colleges and universities which are part of the National Association of Intercollegiate Athletics (NAIA), an administrative body completely independent from the NCAA, and founded in 1940. A handful of these
NAIA schools also compete in the NCAA in some sports. NAIA
schools tend to be small (many with enrollments under 1,000) and
rural and most have limited sports programs. Financial aid, however, is available.

To be accepted into an NAIA member school, an entering freshman must meet *two of the three* entry-level requirements:

1 A minimum score of 18 on the enhanced ACT or 740 on the SAT

2 An overall high school grade point average of 2.0 or higher on a 4.0 scale

3 Graduate in the upper half of the student's high school graduating class

You won't play on national television or before tens of thousands of people at an NAIA school, but you can get a good education and have a fine college experience. And playing professional sports is not impossible. Just ask Scottie Pippen. He attended an NAIA college.

NAIA schools compete in baseball, basketball, cross country, football, golf, soccer, swimming, tennis, track, and wrestling. For the latest information on the NAIA and its member schools, talk to your coach or adviser or contact:

National Association of Intercollegiate Athletics
6120 S. Yale, Suite 1450
Tulsa, OK 74136

NSCAA

The National Small College Athletic Association (NSCAA) was formed in 1966 in order to give its 10 charter members a chance to compete against schools their own size (under 1,000 students). There are now approximately 100 NSCAA schools competing for NSCAA championships in baseball, basketball, cross country, soccer, and track, but some schools may compete in additional sports. For the latest information on the NSCAA, talk to your coach or adviser or contact:

National Small College Athletic Association
113 East Bow Street
Franklin, NH 03235

NCCAA

The National Christian College Athletic Association (NCCAA) was formed 30 years ago to provide, according to its mission statement, "a Christian-based organization that functions uniquely as a national and international agency for the promotion of outreach and ministry, and for the maintenance, enhancement, and promotion of intercollegiate athletic competition in a Christian perspective."

Ninety-four member schools compete for NCCAA championships in baseball, basketball, cross country, soccer, track and field, and wrestling, but some schools may field teams in additional sports. For the latest information on the NCCAA, talk to your coach or adviser or contact:

National Christian College Athletic Association
P.O. Box 1312
Marion, IN 46952

• • • •

By doing your homework about college opportunities and carefully examining what level of academic and athletic achievement will be best for you, you will be able to find a school that is right for you. In the chapters ahead we will help you find a school that is *best* for you.

2 How Good Are You and How Do You Get Coaches to Notice?

You've determined that you want to go to college and may even have some idea where you would like to go. Are you good enough to play there? Will you be happy there? It's time to examine yourself, your abilities, and your motivation to improve and succeed.

Determing Your Level of Ability

Judging talent—especially raw, undeveloped talent—is one of the hardest things to do in sports. Determining a student athlete's level of ability requires Solomon's wisdom and Cassandra's ability to see into the future because you need the skill to judge

- physical talent;
- mental toughness;
- potential;
- how an individual talent will eventually mesh with other individual talents.

19

Rare is the coach who is always right. Rare is the biased parent or adviser who is ever right.

Of the four different judging skills mentioned above, judging physical ability is in some ways the easiest because it is frequently measurable in numbers: athletes can run or swim so fast, lift so much weight, jump so high, et cetera. In track, swimming, diving, and golf, coaches have times or scores to base their opinions on; there are guidelines for judging an athlete's physical ability. Numbers, however, cannot measure an athlete's will to win. And in the team sports, numbers are just part of the equation. It's also important to know what the entire team is like, what the coaching is like, and what the competition is like, among other important factors.

But those are problems the recruiters have to solve. Your task is to determine your own level of ability so that you can best position yourself for the coaches and scouts who can get you to the collegiate level that's best suited for your talents and your goals as both a student and an athlete.

Judging Your Physical Ability

The key factors in virtually every sport are strength, speed, quickness, coordination, and size. Generally speaking, the ideal athlete—except in gymnastics, diving, and sometimes golf—is big, strong, fast, quick, and coordinated. But not everyone is a muscled 220 pounds with the ability to run a 4.4 second 40-yard dash. There is room for the small person in virtually any NCAA sport at virtually any NCAA level, but it's generally a safe bet that, especially in basketball and football, that

- if you're small, you better have big-time skills . . .
- . . . but if you're big, small-time skills might still impress a recruiter.

Put another way, if you're a 5′6″, 160-pound football running back, it's unlikely that Division I college recruiters are going to be begging for your services unless you're faster than lightning. You may have Division I ability, but, unfortunately, you have Division I-AA or Division II size. However, if you're 7′3″ and skinny as a broomstick, a basketball coach might shrug and say, "We'll put some weight on him." If you're big and strong it sometimes doesn't matter if you have hands of stone and feet of concrete. Coaches will only see your upside potential.

A good first step in determining your level of ability is to see how you would fit in sizewise with a college team you would like to play for. But remember to compare yourself to the average player and not the rare exception. Pro basketball players like Mugsy Bogues (5'3") and Spud Webb (5'6") are players who beat the odds with phenomenal quickness and talent to excel in the NBA despite their size. Such odds—and talents—are one in a million. Be realistic.

Five questions to ask yourself to help determine your physical ability:

1 Am I the right size to play the position I now play at the next level?
2 Am I the right size to play another position at the next level?
   Example: With the necessary speed and quickness, a 220-pound lineman in high school could become a linebacker in college. A 6'5" basketball center in high school, with the necessary quickness, ball-handling ability, and shooting range, could become a small forward in college.
3 (In team sports.) How do I perform—in drills and in games—relative to my teammates and my competition? (In nonteam sports.) How does my performance level compare to national and local standards?
4 How do the athletes I'm competing against compare to other athletes at our age level?
5 How do I compare to older, more experienced athletes?

One other important physical attribute to consider, related to quickness, is foot speed. In determining a player's chance to adjust to a higher level, coaches consider foot speed—and lateral movement—very highly. The ability to move side to side, diagonally, and forward to backward are important in virtually every sport and give an excellent clue as to an athlete's ability to play defense—with regard to both how much ground the athlete can cover and how quickly the athlete can get to a spot. Watch any good defensive basketball guard, football cornerback, or baseball shortstop and you'll get an idea of the importance of foot speed. Then ask your coach or phys ed instructor for some drills to help improve it.

Determining Your Mental Toughness

It's difficult enough for coaches to determine physical ability; mental toughness adds in a wild-card factor. It's not physical talent that makes you perform at 110 percent. It's not physical talent that calms your nerves in pressure situations (although it does help). To want the ball at crunch time and perform well in the clutch, be it on the football field, the tennis court, or the balance beam, requires a strong mind and a lot of self-confidence. How does a coach judge that?

One way to show a coach that you have what it takes upstairs is to have a strong work ethic in school. An active mind won't make you jump higher, but the mental discipline required to perform well in the classroom *will* translate over to athletics as well.

Another way to impress a coach that you can perform well under pressure is, obviously, to perform well under pressure—to call for the ball at the ends of games and make big plays when your team needs you. Now, college coaches won't always be there to see all your accomplishments, but word gets out. Let your heroics speak for themselves, but if they don't, prepare a fact sheet touting your achievements.

Another way to impress a coach with your mental abilities is to ask good questions, give good answers, and be eager to talk game strategy and ways that you can improve yourself. If a coach thinks that you're always thinking about your sport and your skills, that coach will think you might have a mental edge in competition.

Last, when meeting coaches, recruiters, and alumni, act like an athlete who knows what's going on. Act like a leader. Hold your head up and speak directly and clearly. Self-confidence is self-confidence no matter where you are.

Estimating Your Potential

Think it's hard to judge mental toughness? Try potential. Try looking at a kid in high school and guessing what he or she is going to be like in four years. Do you remember what you were like four years ago? Can you imagine what you're going to be like four years from now?

It's not that difficult to guess potential with the elite athletes—those with realistic professional or world-class aspirations—but those athletes probably aren't looking at a very long college career, anyway.

For all the rest—all you underachievers *and* overachievers and those performing at the norm—it's pretty much of a crapshoot. Bodies develop differently. Interests change. Priorities change. That's one of the reasons coaches age so quickly—their futures are dependent on the biology and thought processes of a bunch of teenagers.

Hey, it's easy to spot Michael Jordan in a Chicago Bulls uniform. It's not so easy when he's in the 10th grade. And think how many big-name college basketball programs passed on Jordan's all-star teammate Scottie Pippen, who played his college ball at the NAIA's University of Central Arkansas—and averaged only 4.3 points per game as a freshman. David Robinson went to Navy an unheralded 6'5" freshman and graduated a 7' tall all-American. Everybody was recruiting John Elway and Jim Kelly when they went to Stanford and Miami, respectively, but how many coaches sat on the doorstep of Steve McNair, who went to Division I-AA Alcorn State and became an all-American, a Heisman Trophy candidate, and a Houston Oiler. Think of all the great players who are missed by the big-name schools and you'll get an idea of how difficult scouting and recruiting really are. Check the rosters of some of the pro teams in your area and look at the colleges the players came from. Don't be surprised to find that all the footballers did not come from Miami, USC, Michigan, and Notre Dame, and that all the hoops stars are not from UCLA, Duke, Kansas, and North Carolina.

One of the reasons it's so difficult to judge talent at the high school level is because teenage bodies are undergoing such a rapid maturation process. A 6'1", 180-pound junior becomes a 6'4", 210-pound senior. A gangly, seemingly uncoordinated, 6'9" stick figure puts on 20 pounds over the summer and begins to dominate. Athletes who depended on their quickness and agility as high school juniors may find themselves relying on their strength as high school seniors as their bodies continue to fill out. Joe Valerio was recruited to the University of Pennsylvania as a 6'5", 235-pound offensive lineman who also played center on his Ridley High basketball team. He graduated from Penn four years later as a 6'5", 295-pound all-Ivy lineman and a draftee of the Kansas City Chiefs.

Nobody knows how a body will mature, but the big-name, big-time programs have the luxury of not having to guess. These schools generally go after the players who have matured early and who have the physical ability and strength to compete at the college level while still in high school. Fortunately for the many other high schoolers wishing to be recruited, there are but so many of these physical specimens to go around. In addition, what sometimes comes back to haunt the big-time programs is that some of these athletes who've matured early have finished maturing. They peaked in high school. You, on the other hand, may be just getting started.

That's why it's important to not get discouraged in the recruiting process. It is not a terrible setback if you cannot perform at the highest possible level straight out of high school. What is important is that you find yourself at the right level—one in which the athletic competition and the classroom environment will be challenging and enriching. If you and the entire world of college recruiters underestimate your abilities, you can rectify it later by either dominating your competition at the level you're at or transferring to a higher level of play. If, however, you overestimate your abilities coming out of high school or let others swell your head with big ideas and place you at a higher level than you belong, you're likely to get cut from your college team or spend four frustrating years languishing on the bench or quitting.

In that respect, it's important for you to know whether you're the type of athlete who wants to play or wants to watch. It's easy to say you would rather play, but if you have the potential to be a star at some small mid-level college or get a full scholarship to Notre Dame with the understanding that you will almost assuredly ride the pines, it may be hard for you to turn down the prestige and excitement of the Golden Dome. Just make sure you have the mentality to be happy picking splinters.

There's one more thing to consider in some of the outdoor sports, when trying to estimate your potential: the weather. PGA star **Fred Funk** served as head golf coach at the University of Maryland for almost eight years. As the northernmost school in the Atlantic Coast Conference (ACC), coaching a sport in which most of the top players and programs are in the warmer southern climates, Funk tried to use Maryland's weather disadvantages to his advantage while recruiting.

"One way of drawing a southern kid who's not a blue chip recruit is to explain to him how he might get lost in the herd at a southern school. In a northern school, he might have a better chance of starting and becoming exposed to more competition and become a better player a little quicker. That's the one draw for a guy to come to the North from the South and something to consider."

How Your Individual Talent Will Mesh with Team Talents

One other factor that a coach has to consider when assessing your abilities is how you're going to fit into the system the coach plays in college and how your talents will complement the players who are already on the team and the other players being recruited. A team of all all-stars is not a happy team because everybody wants to be a star.

University of Pennsylvania lacrosse coach **Ann Sage,** whose teams have made two trips to the Final Four during her 25 years of coaching lacrosse and field hockey, believes that "the high school athlete who's hardworking and has the ability to improve is the one I'm looking for. I'm not always recruiting a team MVP. Somebody's feeding the ball to that girl. In a team sport, there's got to be someone in the supporting cast. You have your impact players and your feeder players. Players who just get the job done."

So if a coach is in the stands to scout you and you feel as if you're having an off game, try to concentrate on the little things that only a coach might notice. Show the coach that you can be a help to your team even when the spotlight isn't shining on you.

Tips for Showcasing Yourself

Unless you choose to attend college as a student athlete walk-on (someone who tries out for a team without benefit of a scholarship or even serious interest from collegiate coaches), chances are you want to be recruited. Although coaches and university admissions officers have the final say in the recruiting process (coaches frequently wield tremendous power at the sports powerhouses), they are generally not the most important people at the start of the process—scouts, touts, alums, your high school coach, and you are.

Since so much competition occurs during "dead" periods (times when collegiate coaches are prohibited from watching or making contact with student athletes), a number of periodicals for a variety of sports have sprouted up to fill in the gaps. These services are especially helpful to college coaches in basketball and football, where limited staffs, budgets, and available days of allowed travel make it more and more difficult to recruit nationwide. The exception to this would be sports such as golf, swimming, gymnastics, or track, in which individual performance times or scores can be somewhat objective and easily tracked by college coaches and recruiters.

But in the team sports, especially football, in which (a) there are so many players on so many teams, (b) high school skills do not always translate well to college, and (c) the quality of individual play (for linemen, for instance) doesn't always show up on the scoreboard, coaches rely on a variety of sources (local alumni, scouting services, magazines, and newspapers) in order to get tips and track talent. There are just too many fine athletes playing at the high school level for coaches to follow everyone's progress. It is therefore very important to do whatever you can to get yourself noticed. And the sooner the better. Because once you make the list of a scouting service, people start tracking your progress. And since coaches like to identify potential recruits as early in the process as possible, the sooner you can get noticed, the sooner you can get *really* noticed.

Camps and Leagues

Camps and leagues are important because they keep your skills sharp during the off-season, provide opportunities for you to learn from different coaches, allow you to play against varying levels of competition and with different teammates, and, most important, provide more opportunities for recruiters to see you play. The earlier you begin to participate in camps and summer leagues—boys can start playing AAU basketball at the age of 10—especially those that are attended by college coaches, the faster you can begin to make a name for yourself. This is important for three reasons.

1 By gaining a coach's attention early, you increase your options (you get to deal with the coach more frequently and in more detail—enhancing your ability to make the right decision—and one coach's early interest in you occasionally sparks the interest of rival coaches).

2 A coach may be less likely to recruit another athlete at your position if he/she shows early interest in you and you return that interest.

3 If you reach a college decision early, you don't have to worry about the decision during your entire senior year. This gives you the chance to concentrate on winning a championship, your schoolwork, and your social life. Removing the daunting challenge of choosing a college gives many students a great sense of relief.

If, however, you're a late-blooming athlete, making a quick decision may not be in your best interest. You may choose not to jump at the first coach who calls. By waiting to see how the recruiting wars shake out—in which athletes may become ineligible due to academic troubles, for instance, thereby opening up previously taken spots—you may be able to land at a school and a program that is better than you ever could have imagined.

Choosing a Summer League or Camp

A good way to find out about the quality of a summer league, or an AAU team, is to ask local coaches and players. If all the best players in your area are in one league, that gives you a good idea what the quality is like. Ask your high school coach which league is best suited to your level of ability. See where the high schoolers you compete against during the year are going. And call a local collegiate coach—even if you have no interest in his/her school—to find out which league in your area is most respected by college coaches.

When choosing a camp, in any sport, it's important to note the credibility of the people involved, what the program's reputation is like, and, maybe most important, what the competition is like. You don't want to pit yourself against weaker players who you will dominate easily, and you don't want to be embarrassed by top-level players if you're not ready for that level. Given the choice, however, it's better to play against the better players.

Remember, of course, that most of the top camps do their own choosing: if you're a basketball player you can't decide you want to go to Nike—they decide. That's true with the top camps for all the sports.

Ann Sage believes that "camps are good because they give feedback. A girl might make varsity when she's in the ninth grade. Then she goes off to camp and she makes the all-star team (and then human nature is such that with her physical skills recruiters start talking to her), then she continues to develop and by her junior year she starts looking at colleges." Going to a camp can let a burgeoning student athlete see where he/she stands in relation to his/her peers and gives him/her the confidence to pursue the sport further.

Another positive to choosing a camp—if it is a camp attended by coaches during a "live" recruiting period—is that the camp may allow you to be seen by a number of coaches at once. These could be coaches who may actually be at the camp to see someone else but who may be impressed by you, and coaches who will need to see you at a camp (where they can also see a number of other players) because time and budget pressures may prohibit them from traveling to a number of different summer league venues to see you play.

Choosing a camp, however, is not always so simple because there are not only the quality considerations regarding level of play and coaching mentioned above, but also your own travel considerations, money considerations, and "position" considerations. Some camps specialize only in certain areas of a sport—such as a big-man camp in basketball, a quarterback camp in football, or a goalie camp in soccer.

As an AAU basketball coach, Leo Papile obviously favors the AAU system over camps, but his reasoning is worth considering and can certainly be applied to other sports. "The AAU environment is more structured," he says. "At the camps, you're seeing guys who are looking to exhibit more of their individual skills. In AAU ball it's more like high school or college basketball because you're on a team and your role on that team is whatever the coach determines it to be. At camp it's more like every man for himself. Not that the camps are bad—there's pretty good instruction going on there."

Jim Tavarez, an AAU coach for the New Bedford, Massachusetts, team, agrees: "One of the advantages of a kid playing with his own team as opposed to attending a camp is that a kid knows what is going to go on, he knows he's going to get the ball. At a camp, if you get placed on a team with a ball hog, you can be there the whole week just running up and down the court, never getting the ball, and never showing your abilities. It's better to play within a team structure, with people you're familiar with."

Taking the opportunity to play with and against collegiate athletes can also be a big help.

- You can pick up tips and raise your own level of play.
- You can catch the eye of a collegian who will recommend you to his/her coach.

Says Leo Papile: "If you play a young kid who thinks he's 'great' against better, older players who know that they themselves are only 'pretty good,' you get the younger kid to realize that what he's doing right now is only the beginning of his career. Sometimes kids hang around guys who like to pump them up with ideas about how great they are, but I'm one of those guys who likes to knock those ideas out."

It's also important to make a good choice regarding your summer league or camp because these off-season coaches often have a surprising amount of pull with collegiate coaches. And they can help you showcase your all-around abilities by allowing you to play another position or highlight a newly learned skill, which may not be possible on your high school team. It's therefore important to play for someone who will look out for your interests above his/her own.

Leo Papile adds: "A coach's recommendation goes a long way for kids who are solid Division I players but not among the elite players. A recommendation can be the difference between playing and not playing, between going to college on scholarship or paying out of your own pocket . . . If a coach keeps pumping up those gray-area guys—those mid-major prospects—it works, as long as somebody believes in the coach's credibility."

. . . .

One last thing to note about camp invitations: Make sure you and your coach know when the recruiting "dead" periods are. You don't want all your best games to be when coaches aren't allowed to watch you play.

The Importance of Good Grades

Another important factor in getting a good jump on the recruiting process is to be a good student. Coaches want to recruit outstanding students because:

- outstanding students don't have to worry about freshman eligibility
- outstanding students bring up the overall grade point average (GPA) of the athletes on the team
- outstanding students look good in the media guide ("John has a 3.8 GPA and will be attending medical school in the fall")—even if some of these outstanding students never get off the bench to actually play

For this reason, it's not uncommon to see athletic powerhouses join in the recruiting battles for lesser athletes with big-time grades—especially before the start of the senior year. Interest, however, in these brainy athletes, who might be great players at a lower level, frequently diminishes once the coaches find out how their top-priority recruits have scored on their SATs. It's therefore essential to understand your level of ability, know what you want your role to be at college (starter, backup, benchwarmer, fan), and be alert to detect which coaches are recruiting you as a "brain" and not taking you seriously as a ballplayer.

For the outstanding high school baseball player, good grades are important for another reason: leverage. "When you have good grades," says Pete Incaviglia, "a major league baseball team knows that you can go to college, so it makes you a harder person to sign. If you're someone who doesn't do well in school and they know that you can't get into college, then they don't have to do anything. They can wait you out. Especially for a first-round pick, you want to have as many options as you can."

Fortunately, outstanding students who are also outstanding athletes have many top-notch institutions to choose from: Duke, North Carolina, Virginia, Michigan, UCLA, Stanford, California, and Georgetown are all Top-20 universities that field Top-20 teams in one or more sports. And except for football, in which they play in Division I-AA, Ivy League schools frequently compete at a high Division I level in many sports, especially the so-called nonrevenue sports (fencing, crew, lacrosse, field hockey).

Showcasing Your Skills

If you think you have a legitimate chance to be recruited to play college sports, it is important that you have the support and cooperation of your parents (or guardians) and your high school coach. Obviously, it's in the best interests of your coach to see to it that you get as much exposure as possible, but it helps if you show the coach your desire.

So before your season starts, you should sit down with your coach and parents to plan a strategy for dealing with recruiters (see chapter 4) and for showcasing your skills to the best possible advantage. Keep in mind that you must be good enough to showcase, so you have to be honest with yourself about your own abilities. And also remember that if there are other college-level players on your team, you will have to share the spotlight.

If you perform in an individual sport, there are a number of ways a coach can improve your recruitability:

- talking you up to college recruiters via phone calls and letters
- seeing to it that you get invited to the best meets or matches
- scheduling tough in-season competition
- developing strategies for competition that allow you to maximize your own talents and put you in the best position to win, and also allow you to show all facets of your ability

In team sports, the coach can have a far greater impact due to positioning and plays. You might be an outstanding high school quarterback, but too small to play the position in college. A good coach might give you some time at cornerback in order to help you get a scholarship. A coach who's eager to help you might design a few plays to help you look good or give you frequent opportunities to perform. If you've played shooting guard in high school but hope to play point guard in college, you and your coach are going to have to agree that you are going to get ample opportunity to show off your ball handling and passing ability—especially when recruiters are in attendance. If you know a college coach is looking at you to play a different position in college, your high school coach can help you tremendously by letting you get some experience at that position.

Your coach can also help you through scheduling. By playing against well-known teams or teams with prominent players at your position, you can make it easier for college recruiters to scout you—because they're already coming to scout these other players. This is especially true if your high school is in an out-of-the-way area difficult for coaches to get to. Also, in a game against top talent, the coach can also see how you stack up against a player of high quality.

Bill Ellerbee says that "tournaments and games against other high-profile teams provide opportunities not just for the high-profile kids but for the others as well. [Coaches] would come out to see [former Gratz star] Rasheed Wallace, but they'd also get to see younger players. This puts them in recruiters' minds."

Another thing to consider when you try to showcase yourself is the style that you play and the style of the teams that are recruiting you. If you're a drop-back quarterback, you won't get much interest from schools that run the wishbone offense. If your game has a lot of flash, a basketball team that runs a control offense may not have much interest. It's therefore very important to learn about the styles of play of the schools recruiting you. Ask a lot of questions. See as many of their games as you can. Learn what the coach has planned for you. Don't get caught in a situation in which a school is after you primarily because it doesn't want one of its competitors—for whom you might really succeed—to get you. There should be a good fit on both sides.

You might think you're supremely gifted, and you may be for your age and level, but talent at the high school level is extremely raw: Athletes tend to be undisciplined and lacking in the knowledge of their sports' fundamentals. Unfortunately, that is still usually true when the players go on to the collegiate level. It is therefore important to remember that no matter what your style or what your level, there are three things that will always catch a coach's or recruiter's eye:

- attitude
- hustle
- teamwork

Compete with those three things in mind and you'll get noticed.

Your Own Personal Media Kit

Colleges are limited by NCAA rules as to what kind of material they can send you. There are no limits, except for time and money, on what you can send them.

Newspaper articles, game stories, box scores, et cetera are a very good way to keep coaches updated on your progress. If a nice piece appears on you in the local paper, make some copies and send one off to any coach you're trying to interest. It's always good to include a personal letter explaining your interest and why you think you'd be a good fit in that coach's program.

Game films and personal performance videos are also great ways to show your stuff, and it's becoming much more common to use them in the recruiting wars—especially for students who can afford them. An official copy of a game film is certainly acceptable, and many students send tapes their parents, guardians, or friends record from the stands. Quality, of course, varies greatly; the important thing is that you play well. Some industrious student athletes will even edit together their own personal highlights tapes if they're extremely eager to get a coach's attention.

Don't, however, try to fake a coach out with a package that's all style but no substance. Ann Sage warns that most coaches won't fall for it. "Just because a résumé is attractive and a player has five pages on themself doesn't mean they're good."

Stay Level-Headed

Pete Incaviglia says that you have to keep a level perspective when you're playing before scouts and college coaches and not get too up or down depending on how well you play. "In baseball, it's hard to showcase people. When I was first playing, you hardly ever saw a scout in the stands at one of our high school games. And you don't play that many games. So if a scout comes down and you have a bad game, you're labeled 'not a player' and you could be a great player. You see guys drafted in the thirty-second round who are better than guys drafted in the second round. If you have ability somewhere along the line you're going to get noticed. But luck has a lot to do with it."

Still, you can work to improve your luck. Showcasing yourself does not mean you should act cocky or be a hot dog. There's a fine line between being an intense competitor and being an arrogant jerk, and you must find that line for yourself if you're to succeed. Coaches like athletes who support their team, play hard, and play to win. They like athletes who are nice when they're not playing, but not so nice when they are playing. They don't like athletes who dog it, play hard only in spurts, and look like they're only out for themselves. They don't like athletes who are constantly in trouble. College coaches have enough to do: They don't want to have to get you out of jams. No matter how good you are, if you look like a head case, someone who might disrupt team chemistry, coaches are going to stay away. So in addition to showcasing your athletic abilities, it's important to showcase your nonathletic abilities. Are you friendly? Honest? Hard-working? Do you take practice seriously? Do you look to improve? Do you take your schoolwork seriously? Are you active in extracurricular activities?

It's important to show coaches, especially if you're a borderline recruit, that you're going to be a decent person to have at school, in the locker room, on the team bus, and on the playing field. Think about what's best about your personality and showcase that.

Recommendations

If Division I coaches do not call shortly after they're allowed by NCAA rules to start calling, it is important for you, the student athlete to become proactive. Call them. Make yourself accessible. Show interest. It's possible that your name may have slipped through the cracks, and it's also possible that your enthusiasm may impress the coach or that he/she will recommend you to another coach if you are not quite right for his/her program. All coaches in a sport know each other (they're always traveling to the same places, meeting at the same camps and/or conventions, and networking for the same jobs), and many of them have worked with each other at previous jobs, so it's quite common for coaches to recommend potential recruits to each other. So while you may not be good enough to play basketball for North Carolina, football for USC, or baseball for Texas, a word from Dean Smith or John Robinson or Augie Garrido, or one of their assistants, could go a long way toward getting you recruited somewhere else.

In addition, by contacting the school, you can quickly gauge their interest. It's better to know early than late that your top choices aren't really interested in recruiting you. That gives you more time to reexamine your options and plan a new strategy.

3 Preparing Yourself for the Big Leap to College

Now that you've started to consider how good an athlete you are, what level of collegiate play you want to try for, and how to market yourself to those coaches and recruiters, it's time to look inside and start considering how to improve yourself.

Preparing Yourself Academically

Every year at signing time the newspapers are filled with sad stories about student athletes who don't make the required SAT score or don't have the necessary GPA in their core courses to accept an athletic scholarship to a Division I program. Whether these NCAA rules for admission are fair is an issue for another book—the point is that these are the rules and as you will learn throughout life, not all rules are fair. One thing, however, that is fair about the NCAA rules is that they are not secret, like so many rules you will encounter later in life. The NCAA's academic guidelines are publicly announced, endlessly debated, and heavily advertised with handouts, public service spots on television, and word-of-mouth from coaches and advisers. So there is no reason for a student athlete to not be prepared academically when the time comes to make a decision about college.

University of Georgia basketball star Saudia Roundtree had a fine high school transcript but didn't do well on the SATs and was forced to go to junior college, where she excelled both on the court and in the classroom, before becoming an all-American at Georgia. Her story is all too common: "I didn't make any bad grades in high school," she says, "I was always an A, B, or C student. I just didn't test well and I still don't understand how they base what you did in four years on one test."

But knowing that those are the rules makes Roundtree wonder why more student athletes don't get their academics in order. "Some of these kids are so naïve," Roundtree says. "They think 'it's not going to happen to me.' It's like AIDS—a lot of people just go out and do stuff and say 'It's not going to happen to me. I'm invincible.' But then they can't go to the college of their choice because they didn't do anything academically. It's still happening. You see great great players who don't do anything in school and then when it's time to sign, they can't go to the school that they want to go to."

To make sure that you are on track to meet the necessary requirements of the schools in which you're interested, you should talk to the coaches at those schools and your own academic adviser(s). Go over your grade point average, the courses you've taken and the courses you plan to take in your senior year. Discuss when you plan to take the SAT and/or the ACT and find out what score you need to hit on these standardized tests in order to adequately complement your high school grades.

After that, get yourself an SAT/ACT prep book or enroll in a prep class if you can afford it. If you can't afford it, talk to your coach or adviser about free tutoring that might be available through your school.

Your high school and/or club coach should be an asset in this process. AAU Coach Leo Papile says that the first thing he does with the players on his team "is a thorough examination of the transcript to see exactly where they are in terms of the number of courses they've passed, what courses they've passed, and if there's a deficiency you want to see what the deficiency is.

"It's very easy to find an alternative—going back and repeating the year, getting all the bugs out. Taking the courses you failed over. It's only one year out of your life and if you graduate at nineteen instead of eighteen it's no big deal. Sometimes you find that a private education might solve those problems a little better because they have more individualized attention. So find the problem, eliminate the problem, and go on to a new area, maybe in a different school environment."

Once you feel that you're where you need to be in terms of the admissions process, you should get an idea as to where you and your high school education will fit into the overall student body. If the school you want to go to is stretching to admit you because of your athletic abilities, you must prepare yourself for classrooms and classwork that will be difficult to handle. Ask the coaches recruiting you if their schools offer prefreshman academic programs and find out what courses will be required of you during your freshman year so you can try to get a jump on the coursework. Also, you should do as much extra reading as possible during your senior year and through the summer. You want your study and concentration skills honed to their highest levels when you start college.

Craig Conlin played college basketball at La Salle University with four players, including Lionel Simmons and Tim Legler, who later played in the NBA. He now is a high school football, baseball, and basketball coach at Germantown Academy, a fine suburban Philadelphia prep school. His attitude about academic preparation is no different from his attitude about life preparation. "The key is developing a work ethic," he says, "and trying your best. Give it everything you have no matter what you do. That comes from my parents and my dad harping, 'If you're going to be a ditchdigger, you better be the best there is in the world.' That carries over into academics, into everything."

Last, Penn Relays director Dave Johnson reminds high school athletes that "a college recruiter is looking for someone who doesn't have to be coddled all through college and looked over to make sure they're going to class and getting their studies done. Probably the biggest pain in the neck to any college coach is having to worry about his kids' grades. On the other hand, they have to be concerned with

that. An athlete isn't going to do them any good, if they're ineligible."
So get your study habits in order and make sure that the coaches recruiting you know that your study habits are in order.

Preparing Yourself Athletically

Collegiate athletes are bigger, better, stronger, and older than high
school athletes, so if you are going to reach your potential and excel
at the collegiate level, you are going to need to improve your
strength, your endurance, your knowledge, and your skill.

In terms of improving your knowledge of your sport and the
competition level at the colleges to which you're applying, Dave
Johnson says that the high school student athlete is mostly reliant on
his/her coach. "But beyond that, I think it comes down to reading.
You've got to be aware of what's out there in the sport—you've got to
be aware of the sport. Become a fan of the sport. Some of the best
athletes I've known were pretty dumb about their sport. They had a
very narrow view of what they had to do. They didn't have a very
strong sense of reality, which meant they sometimes were very frus-
trated about not being able to achieve what they wanted to achieve.
The other side of the same coin is that they didn't realize that they
were on the verge of accomplishing something that most people
would have said was beyond their abilities. Athletics is doing what
you haven't been able to do before and one of the worst things you
can do is limit yourself with your own mind. On the other hand, your
mind has to temper what can be done."

So in terms of the mental preparation, you should set high goals
for yourself and see how your abilities, should you reach your goal,
will fit into the programs of the colleges you're considering. These
goals should definitely include a serious fitness regimen, so ask the
coaches who are recruiting you what you need to do to get into
college-level condition. Take the workouts they give you and, with the
help of your high school coach and/or a local fitness trainer, devise a
workout that will help you maximize your potential and make those

first few practices of your college career, when other freshman are wilting around you, a bit more bearable.

Women's "Dream Team" member **Jennifer Azzi**, of Stanford, recommends "a good weight training program and some kind of running program, because one of the things that really holds people back, especially girls, are injuries. The stronger you are and the more in shape you are, for any sport, the less likely you are to get injured. The biggest transition in any sport is the level of strength. The people in college are so much stronger."

But the high school student athlete also has to be concerned about trying to improve too quickly. It takes time for muscles, muscle memory, and technique to develop. "One of the worst things an athlete can do is try to do too much," says Dave Johnson. Using track's triple jump, an event that requires athletic ability and technique, as an example of what can happen if you try to go beyond what you're realistically capable of doing, Johnson says, "If you extend too far on a triple jump, you end up breaking down instead of getting a better jump out of it." It's an important lesson to keep in mind.

An excellent way to continue to improve your athletic ability, says Johnson, is to always think you have to prove yourself. "Show that you care," he says. "Put as much effort into what you're doing as you can. Make certain that you're trying—but if you look like you're a phony, people are going to spot you as a phony. If you're doing calisthenics, do them fully. If it's a big team, you want to be up near the front of the pack. Always try to constantly improve."

Preparing Yourself Socially

When Pennsylvania lacrosse coach Ann Sage makes a recruiting trip, determining a player's skill level, academic abilities, and, of course, interest, are only some of the pieces of the puzzle. Another is the player's behavior.

"When I'm visiting a recruit," Sage says, "I watch the interaction between the parent and child. I watch a lot of things. I like a humbleness in an individual. A quiet individual. I don't like someone to come in here and tell me how good they are. Most of your outstanding athletes don't run their mouths about who they are or what they've done."

On the playing field, Sage says she looks for a first step, quickness, speed, and various intangibles. But off the field she looks for honesty in an individual. "I look for integrity," she says, "how they treat their peers. I can't have a discipline problem. I can't have a big mouth. They create such turmoil."

As you can see, your social maturation for college doesn't start when you step on campus at the start of your freshman year. From the time coaches start watching you play, writing you letters, and visiting you at school or home, your actions and behavior will be under a microscope. Unless your talent level is off the charts, coaches do not like to take chances on troublemakers. Their jobs are at stake. So almost as if you are a political candidate, you have to sell the coaches who are recruiting you on your character. Coaches will always recruit character.

How do you show that you have character? Extracurricular work for a charity or religious organization is a good sign, but you don't have to do anything above and beyond these 10 simple rules.

1   Go to school.
2   Stay out of trouble.
3   Practice and play hard.
4   Do not mouth off to officials or referees.
5   Do not mouth off to your coach.
6   Do not mouth off to your teammates.
7   Play hard when the game is on the line.
8   No fighting.
9   Show respect to your parents, guardians, and other adults.
10   Be polite.

With your character checklist completed, it's time to consider some of the other social adjustments you will have to make when you head off to college. These adjustments involve your maturity, your relationships, your attitude, your views, your "look," and your interpersonal skills.

We're not in any way advocating that you change your personality or change the essence of what makes you *you*, but college is the next step on your path to adulthood and you don't still want to be looked upon as irresponsible, as out of touch, or as a kid. It will be important for you to find some kind of niche for yourself in college even while you try retain your own individualism and carve out your own identity.

Because student body culture (what's cool, what's not cool) varies from region to region and school to school, you will need to be *at* college in order to see what you need to change *for* college, but while it may not be beneficial to change before you get to school, it's beneficial to prepare yourself for change.

Image

In high school, you were a big fish in a small pond. Your image was that of a successful student athlete and you were something of a celebrity at school, at home, and in your neighborhood. College is going to enlarge your small community and, for all but the superstar athletes, it will diminish your stature within that community.

Without their family to anchor them and the adoration of their classmates to continually boost their self-esteem, many young collegians try to reinvent themselves. The old persona, no matter how popular and successful, was a high school persona, so freshmen student athletes frequently set out to create a college persona. They shave their heads, change their drinking habits, listen to new kinds of music, experiment sexually or with drugs, change the way they speak, and/or join a fraternity or sorority in order to try to gain a connection to some larger entity and support group. Some of these changes are about finding oneself and are basic to the process of growing up. Others (drinking, drugs, etc.) are merely harmful ways of trying to fit in or trying to escape from the uncomfortable nature of having to deal with change.

One area where many student athletes attempt to define themselves is in their "jock"-ness—either by heightening their "dumb jock" persona (stereotyped by dressing in sweats, chugging brews, getting a Mohawk haircut, shouting obscenities, refraining from intellectual activities, and hanging exclusively with fellow jocks) or by diminishing their jock persona with sportier clothes, eyeglasses, and a demeanor more akin to a professor than a linebacker.

College is a time of change for most students—many of whom are experiencing freedom from parental decision making for the first time—and for the student athlete who's facing added sport-related time commitments and stress, the need to find a peer group is even more essential. But it is important that you not waste time on extracurricular activities, or with "peers," who merely distract you from your goals. It's also important that you not waste energy projecting an image that's not who you are. Do not get caught up in what others (teammates, classmates, fans, alums) think of you. The only opinions that matter are yours, your loved ones, your professors, and your coaches. As long as you do what is expected of you (in the classroom and within your sport) you will project a good image and be well respected.

To help you stay on an even keel, it is essential to have friends, parents, guardians, relatives, coaches, or advisers who you can talk to about what you're thinking and what you're going through. A person who can give you a reality check may be the most important person with regard to your collegiate experience.

Your image will also be a public image (see chapter 9), and you need to keep that in mind at all times. Like it or not, you're a symbol. Don't bully others and don't abuse your celebrity status. It will come back to haunt you.

Freedom

For many student athletes, one of the biggest social changes that will occur in college pertains to individual freedom. You can come and go as you please. You can study when you want. If you want. You can stay up all night and sleep all day (not advised).

Use your freedom to grow and mature, but use it wisely. Don't take advantage of it because, like everything good for you that you abuse, it can turn bad quickly. With freedom come responsibilities.

Quotes from two men whom you should make it a point to read during your college years make this point quite clear.

"Those who expect to reap the blessing of freedom must . . . undergo the fatigue of supporting it."

—Thomas Paine, "The American Crisis," 1776

"Liberty means responsibility. That is why most men dread it."

—George Bernard Shaw, "Maxims for Revolutionists," *Man and Superman*, 1903

Relationships

Here is where freedom has its biggest impact. Living on your own, relationships—be they serious, soul-searching friendships, love interests, crushes, or even one-night stands (not recommended)—will have a chance to develop as never before. Here again it is essential for the student athlete to act responsibly and *never* use one's celebrity or (for men) physical strength to gain a sexual advantage. This type of behavior can end your college career, land you in jail, and ruin your life.

But before we go into on-campus relationships, let's look at the long-distance relationship—a staple for many freshman athletes. It's tough to leave behind a high school sweetheart but unless your high school sweetheart, enrolls at college with you, you are going to be separated. That doesn't mean you have to break up, but it does mean your relationship is going to have to change. Patience and understanding are key here: Don't forget that the new status is equally tough on the person back home or attending his/her own different new college environment.

Talk on the phone a lot (or as much as you can afford), but never use a phone or phone card that is not yours. You can lose your eligibility and get your team put on probation. If you're not too far apart, try to visit each other on occasional weekends. No matter how strong your bond was in high school, there are numerous new distractions at college and it's completely understandable for someone who still cares for you to think that you will soon lose interest in them. If this is not the case, and your feelings run deep even after you've been apart for awhile, you must stress this repeatedly. Showing that you care will make the other person feel a lot better and a lot more secure.

On the other hand, people change when they're at college and what made someone so attractive to you in high school may not be that attractive anymore. At that point, it's important that you communicate openly and honestly with your high school girlfriend/boyfriend. Do not string them along. Do not lie to them. It's extremely difficult to make a long-distance relationship work when your interests and experiences are changing so rapidly. The important thing is to be kind and caring when you discuss breaking up. This person has done nothing to hurt you, and it's possible that after meeting and dating new people you'll decide that this person was the right one after all.

However, should you be the one to *receive* the breakup call when you're not prepared for it, it's important to be honest with your feelings. Don't simmer and stew. Talk to your roommates, teammates, parents, or coaches. With all the changes going on around you, a breakup can be devastating. If necessary, get counseling from a trained professional. There is sure to be someone at your college or university experienced in handling these situations who will keep everything you say in the strictest confidence. It's tough, but don't let the breakup of a longtime relationship get the best of you and hinder your chances for success in school.

If dealing with a long-distance relationship is tough, dealing with on-campus relationships can be tougher. Developing a crush on a classmate can send you into a tailspin—always wondering what they're doing, who they're with, if they like you. You're afraid to approach them with your feelings because every time you see them with someone else you get a pain in the pit in your stomach, but you're also afraid to approach them because you fear the worst. Facing rejection at college can be especially difficult because you might come into contact with the person who rejected you many times a day.

Relating to someone who has developed a crush on you can also be difficult—you want to be sensitive to their feelings, but probably have no experience dealing with such a situation. Again, there are counseling options open to you. Don't be embarrassed to get help. And should a situation develop in which someone you've rejected refuses to stop pursuing you, get help right away. The person hounding you needs help and "stalker" situations can turn very ugly very quickly.

Many of you will have had a sexual relationship before you get to college, but many of you will not. Your experience, or lack thereof, will be a concern to you, and sexual experience is something that men—more so than women, who are more open about their feelings—find difficult to talk over with teammates, who all want to outdo each other in "manliness." If you have an unbelievably understanding coach, you might be able to talk about some of your fears with him/her, but most coaches do not want to help you get through adolescence and most of them would not be very good at it, either. In these cases, you need to depend on close friends, especially longtime friends from home who've grown up with you, parents or guardians, siblings (if you have them), a campus counselor, and the person with whom you're having the relationship. If this person really cares about you, he/she will try to make you feel comfortable. And you should try to make your friend feel comfortable, as he/she is probably experiencing the same feelings. The only universal advice we can give regarding sexual relationships is:

- don't rush
- do not be forced into anything you do not feel you're ready for
- do not feel compelled to compromise any religious principles you might have regarding premarital sex
- make sure you are both absolutely, unequivocally, inarguably ready to take your relationship to this new level
- use protection to save yourself from an unwanted pregnancy or the passing on of sexually transmitted diseases

The reason that you must always make sure that you and your partner are always 100 percent sure that you want to engage in a sexual relationship is that one of the ugliest situations for the student athlete—and one of the most common—pertains to rape or sexual assault. It seems as if not a week goes by in which some high school or college athlete is not being hauled into a police station for some sex crime. Whether it's mob mentality and too much liquor leading to sex with an unwilling or unresponsive young woman or jealousy and anger leading to the punching of one's girlfriend or boyfriend, there's no justifiable excuse for violence. No matter how drunk with lust or power you are, or how upset you are with your boyfriend/girlfriend, this type of behavior is intolerable and illegal.

You have to keep control of your emotions. Do not let rage or pride get the best of you. If you have something burning inside you that makes you want to injure or take sexual advantage of the opposite sex, get help before it gets you in trouble. The drunk or drugged woman being passed around to you at some late-night party is a classmate of yours. She's somebody's daughter or sister. She could be your sister. Show some respect for her and for yourself.

If you see a sexual situation developing in which both parties are clearly not willing or even conscious of what they're doing, step in and stop it and face the consequences. One, two, or more of the people involved may be mad at you at the time, but when morning comes and the dust settles, your friends will thank you. And if they don't? Get new friends.

Last, having a girlfriend or boyfriend or a close friend of the opposite sex can be a wonderful thing—just as it may have been for you in high school. You'll be under enough stress with your schoolwork and your sport. Having a close confidant who can study with you, lift your spirits when you're down, and help you relieve some of that stress can be invaluable. Choose carefully and wisely and hope that the person you choose chooses you back.

Staying in Touch with Friends and Family Back Home

Off at school, on your own and immersed in new and challenging activities, it's often easy to take for granted your friends and relatives back home. If you're homesick or uncomfortable in your new surroundings this won't be a problem—you'll constantly be writing letters, talking on the phone, and going home to visit. But if your newfound freedom agrees with you and you're constantly stimulated by your new surroundings, you may begin to consider your home and your hometown as old, boring news. Get those thoughts out of your mind now.

It's important to your future success that you remember and respect where you came from. The people who love you and support you deserve to know how you're doing and that you're thinking about them. Should you get in trouble and need help down the road, these are the people who will be there for you. They're the base of your support. Make sure that your loved ones get a copy of your game schedule and that they understand ticket availability. If you compete in a sport that has games on radio or television, make sure you inform them when and where the games will be on. Mom, Dad, or some other friends and relatives might go to a sports bar if their child's game is on the satellite. Find out if there are ways for them to travel with the team or stay at the team's hotel on trips to faraway road games should they wish to attend—sure they can stay somewhere else, but the team generally gets a great rate on its airfare and hotel rooms. If the campus paper or a local paper writes an article about you—no matter how small—make sure you get a few copies to mail home. And be sure to call home after every game and let them know how you've done. They'll love you for it, and on days you and/or your team don't play particularly well, you'll appreciate their love even more.

4

What to Consider during the Recruiting Process

Your mailbox is starting to fill up with letters and brochures from colleges around the country and your phone is ringing at all hours with calls from interested coaches. What do you do? Your mailbox is empty and no one is calling. What do you do?

The Dos and Don'ts of Recruiting

The pressure to win in college sports—not to mention the money involved—is so great, that, unfortunately many coaches and programs try to bend the rules in order to gain an advantage. They do things that, although not expressly forbidden, clearly make one question the ethics involved. Even worse, sometimes there are no ethics involved. Too many coaches either knowingly disregard the rules or avert their eyes while assistants, alumni boosters, or local merchants disregard the rules entirely. For the athlete at the top rung of the high school ladder in the revenue-producing sports like football and basketball, stories of bribes, cash gifts, and cars are sadly the norm rather than the exception.

But most athletes don't get to play "Let's Make a Deal." They are recruited in the traditional way—with letters, phone calls, and visits from coaches. Rules violations, however, can still occur even in these recruiting processes because many coaches either don't follow the rules or don't know all the rules—the NCAA manual is, after all, the size of a small city's phone book.

In order to avoid being caught violating recruiting rules and thereby costing yourself eligibility and your team probation, you should carefully read appendix A, page 189, and make yourself aware if the schools recruiting you have any history of rules violations, *and* have a long talk with your high school coach before the recruiting process begins. Learn:

- when the recruiting "dead" periods are (a dead period is when college coaches may not see you play and may not have any contact with you)
- when the evaluation periods are
- how many times coaches are allowed to contact you
- how coaches are allowed to contact you

Your coach should be able to answer these questions and give you advice about other issues to know or avoid. Your coach should also provide you with information and forms for *certification* with the NCAA's Initial-Eligibility Clearinghouse. **If you intend to participate in Division I or II athletics as a freshman, you must register and be certified.** There is no cost to register. If your coach cannot provide you with the proper registration forms, the clearinghouse can be contacted by phone at 319-337-1492.

For more detailed information about recruiting basics, you should also contact the NCAA at 6201 College Boulevard, Overland Park, Kansas 66211-2422 (phone: 913-339-1906). General recruiting regulations (Divisions I, II, and III) from the 1996–1997 guide state:

You become a "prospective student-athlete" when you start ninth-grade classes. Before the ninth grade, you become a prospective student-athlete if a college gives you (or your relatives or friends) any financial aid or other benefits that the college does not provide to prospective students generally.

You become a "recruited prospective student-athlete" at a particular college if any coach or representative of the college's athletic interest (booster or representative) approaches you (or any member of your family) about enrolling and participating in athletics at that college. Activities by coaches or boosters that cause you to become a recruited athlete are:

- providing you with an official visit
- placing more than one telephone call to you or any other member of your family, or
- visiting you or any other member of your family anywhere other than the college campus

The *NCAA Guide* goes into greater depth than we have room for here (see appendix A), but some of its key points are paraphrased below—they will give you an idea as to how easy it is to unwittingly violate NCAA rules.

- When you are a high school student (or a potential college transfer) and you visit a school either officially or unofficially, you may not try out—or be asked to try out—for the college's athletic teams.

- You can visit a college any time at your own expense. On such a visit, you may be provided with up to three free tickets for an athletic contest and you may be taken on a tour of campus and campus facilities, but the tour may not travel beyond 30 miles from campus.

- As a senior, you may accept an offer for an official visit to a school that is recruiting you. An official visit is one in which the school pays for your round-trip travel from your home or high school to campus and provides you with meals, a place to stay, and free tickets to campus sports events—as long as those tickets are in the general seating area and not any type of special seating. Your parents or guardians may also participate in your official visits, but you should check with individual coaches as to what will be provided to them. During your official visit, you may be provided with a student host to help you (and your family) learn more about campus life. This student host may spend up to $30 per day to cover *all* aspects of entertainment for you and your family (so don't expect lobster and the opera), but the $30 cannot be used to purchase any souvenirs or team logo athletic gear at the school's bookstore. Your official visit may not last more than 48 hours.

You may visit no more than five schools on official visits no matter how many sports you are being recruited in. You are not eligible for an official visit unless you have provided the school with a copy of your academic transcript and an official score from the PSAT, SAT, a PACT Plus, or an ACT.

The Role of Your High School, AAU, or Club Coach in the Recruiting Process

Your coach is a very important person in the recruiting process, both as an adviser and as a first line of defense. If your coach is doing his or her job and is concerned with your future as an athlete and a student, he or she should be willing to sit down with you and map out a strategy for dealing with recruiters. Your coach should also be able to provide knowledge and insight into the coaches recruiting you and the teams and schools these coaches represent—you want your coach to help you understand the way their teams play. Your coach also needs to help you understand the politics of recruiting and make sure you don't end up in a situation that's not suited to your abilities and interests.

According to Detroit Pistons coach **Doug Collins**, himself a parent of two college athletes, your coach can also point you toward a school that might be a good match for you. "There are so many scouting services out there now that if you can play, people are going to know about you," Collins says. "There are very few secrets. There are always people who are going to come through late because they're late developers. But if you have a good high school coach or athletic director who really works for the students to help them, those things really help. It happened with my daughter. The assistant coach in her high school played in the Patriot League and felt Kelly could play in the Patriot League so she sent a bunch of tapes to Lehigh and Lafayette and some of those schools, and my daughter ended up at Lehigh."

As a student athlete, you can also take that type of proactive approach to your recruiting, Collins says. "You can write letters to coaches asking them if you can send them tapes of you playing and if they would watch the tapes and let you know if there is any interest on their part."

At the beginning of the recruiting process it is important for your parental advisers and coaches to talk to each other and divide up the responsibilities involved in your recruiting. If you are a student athlete who is going to be heavily recruited, there will be a lot of work to do—sorting through mail, taking and answering phone calls, coordinating in-school, in-house, and official visits, and meaningfully discussing the pros and cons of your possible choices. You are going to have to do the bulk of the work, but those who are close to you in the process should help. Here are some questions to consider as you divide up the possibilities.

● *Do you want your coach or parents to take the initial calls from collegiate recruiters?* If you are the type of athlete who is going to be bombarded with calls, you will probably want your coach (or coach's office) to handle initial calls. If your parents have set up some restrictions as to the quality of schools they will allow you to consider, you may want your parents to answer the phone. Either way, it's probably best if a coach talks to someone else before he/she talks to you.

● *Who is going to research the schools recruiting you?* You can either divide up the schools you're considering between your parents and your coach or you can divide up their responsibilities. We recommend the latter. As you start the weeding-out process, ask your coach to help you review the athletic side of things and ask your parents (or an academic adviser) to help you review the academics. Of course, you should do as much of your own research as possible.

● *How will you weigh the advice you receive when you plan to narrow down your choices?* Consider at the beginning whose opinion is going to hold the most sway with you. Do you expect your coach to help you make the best possible choice for you or does he/she have his/her own agenda? Do your parents and/or guardians really understand how important your sport is to you? Is everybody working from the same playbook?

The Role of Your Parent or Guardian in the Recruiting Process

The most important advisers in the recruiting process, however, should be your parents and/or guardians. If they can put your best interests at heart and avoid temptations of prestige, fame, and/or money for themselves, they should be able to provide you with perspective and the wisdom of age and not allow you to be suckered by fancy talk and empty promises. It is important, though, to try to understand your parents' motivations—they're human, too, and can just as easily get swelled heads from the attention you might be receiving—and to talk it out with them when your goals and theirs seem to be in conflict. Watch out for "stage parent" syndrome, when you begin to feel that your parents' desire for your success is more a reflection on their desire to live vicariously through you as opposed to what may be best for you. No matter how good the intentions of your parents/guardians may be, and we'll just have to assume that their intentions are good, you do not want to let their agenda unduly influence what it is you hope to accomplish with your college choice.

Dave Johnson says that in discussing these issues with your parents/guardians and your coach, it's essential to keep in mind the two parties' concerns. "Sometimes the two groups wind up at opposite poles," says Johnson. "The parent is often looking at a combination of factors. Generally it comes down to finding the best education for the money and that's a mix that the coach probably can't assess well. That comes down to family finances. Coaches are looking for a place where a kid can succeed athletically. What the kid needs to do is talk to both sides and figure out a middle ground."

Longtime Simon Gratz High School basketball coach Bill Ellerbee says, however, that it's very helpful for the coach to have a good relationship with the parent/guardian. "It's easier when you have a relationship," Ellerbee says, "because then you can tell the parents what the kid has to do in order to achieve his college goals. You can tell kids every day—ten times a day—that they have to do their homework, but in the long run, it's the parents who have to make them do it, if they don't have the discipline themselves."

"The parents have to ask the hard questions," says former NBA star and former Maryland congressman **Tom McMillen**. "They should be the ones who put their imprimatur on the selection process. It's very important that they just don't leave it to the kid because a kid can be sold, and I think the parents should avoid allowing them to be sold."

Joseph and Mary Conlin of Philadelphia had to help five different highly recruited athletic children avoid being sold. Sons Chris, Keith, and Kevin each chose to play football at Penn State. Daughter Kimberly played basketball at Philadelphia Textile. And another son, Craig, played basketball at La Salle. Here is his story of his parents' involvement in the recruiting process.

"The basketball coach that I had in high school really didn't play that much of a role in my recruiting," Conlin says. "He felt that it was his duty to get the other guys on the team taken care of for college because he knew I was going to get a Division I scholarship and that he really didn't have to worry about me. He was more worried about everybody else on the team.

"My parents never came out and said it but I always felt that they wanted the kids to go to school locally. If they needed to they wanted to be able to jump in a car and see you within three to four hours—not a plane trip away. But what my father and mom always told me was to put everything on a sheet of paper, pros and cons, what we like and what we don't like. My parents actually made some of the visits that I took. They went down to Richmond with me. They went down to William and Mary with me. So it wasn't as if the coaches were just recruiting me, they were also recruiting my folks."

Like many coaches, especially at the better schools that put a premium on education, Ann Sage, women's lacrosse coach at the University of Pennsylvania, admits to recruiting the folks. "I recruit the mother and father, not the seventeen- or eighteen-year-old," Sage says. "The kids are very impressionable. But the parents, they talk education. If you want to major in a sport as opposed to get an education, then a top school isn't the place for you. I think you have to hit the seventeen- or eighteen-year-old almost in the head and say 'Wake up!' If ten percent play college sports what percent make the pros. You've got to get them out of thinking that everyone is going to get scholarships. Very few get scholarships. The ones that do are the elite athletes."

But one of the problems that Sage has encountered while talking to parents is seeing the increasing pressure they're putting on their children in order to succeed in sport at the highest level possible—in quest of the almighty scholarship. "If the parents have no money," she says, "they've started putting pressure on the child way back in elementary school.

"The expectations are too high and one of the major things that is happening is that we're taking the fun and enjoyment out of sports. Now you have parents walking around carrying video cameras and water buckets—and we're in a rat race right now."

This "rat race" for scholarship money forced Olympic gold medal swimmer **Cristina Teuscher** to face a difficult choice. Clearly among the nation's elite swimmers coming out of high school—she was, after all, on the U.S. Olympic team—Teuscher had scholarship offers from the top swimming programs in the country. But she wanted to stay closer to her New York home and continue training with her club coach, John Collins. After much consultation with her parents, she ended up spurning the scholarships for a nonscholarship Ivy League school, Columbia University.

"That was a big choice," Teuscher says. "Did I really want to put that on my parents to pay for a school like Columbia? We discussed it a lot and they said that they would support me all the way if this is what I wanted to do."

Teuscher's view of the role of the parent: "I think the parents should definitely leave it up to the child to decide and offer all the support they can and tell the child how far they can go in supporting the child and what they're looking for in a school so that the child has an idea but doesn't base the decision solely on what the parents want. I think also the parents should be very understanding of what the kid is looking for."

Olympic fencer **Peter Cox**, a four-time all-American at Penn State, echoes Teuscher's comments. "Your parents should be supportive and they should help give guidance—because I don't believe that your high school helps in that realm enough. My parents were very relaxed and let me choose what I wanted, but I wasn't educated enough in school selection. As a senior in high school, there are a lot of things going through your mind about what type of school you're looking for. And then you get all this information thrown at you and you need someone to help you sift through it and sort it out—for me, that was both academically and fencing-wise. I think your parents and coach have to work together."

Doug Collins was a college basketball star, an NBA star, a successful college assistant coach at Penn and Arizona State, and a successful NBA head coach with the Chicago Bulls and now with the Detroit Pistons, where he coaches Duke great Grant Hill. Ironically, his son Chris played with Hill at Duke, so Collins brings the perspective of a player, a coach, and a parent to the recruiting process.

"Every player you hear talk," Collins says, "you ask them what's the most important thing and they say academics. Well, you know in 99.9 percent of the cases the kid's first interest is where can I go to get the best basketball or whatever sport you're going to play. Then let me make sure the academics is good and hopefully I fit in socially. To me those are the three things that have to be in play for you to make your choice.

"When you're a father," Collins continues, "you talk to your kids and say, 'Look, basketball's important but you've got to take the coach out of the equation. You can't go to a school because of the coach because that coach could leave tomorrow and if they do, do you like the school.' You talk about those three factors that I talked about being important—the opportunity to play, the academics, and the social. I've always felt as an athlete that where you have to have those three things fulfilled to have a happy college life, as a normal student you only have to have two—the social and the academics. But as an athlete, if any of these three things get out of whack you're not going to be happy in college. Most importantly, if you go somewhere where you're not going to play, regardless of whether the other things are good, you're not going to be happy with your decision because you've really only got four years to play.

"So it's a tough decision for a kid because especially if you're a prime-time recruit and all of a sudden the Mike Kryszewskis and the Dean Smiths and the John Thompsons start coming in your home as a seventeen-year-old person your head can start swimming pretty easily.

"When Chris would come back from his visits, I knew exactly what was going to happen—he was going to be on fire for that particular school because that's the last one he saw. The last taste you have is the one that's important, the one that feels the best at that particular moment. And what I always used to do, I would say tell me what you liked about it, tell me what you didn't like, let's talk about the pros and the cons, let's keep a list here of things as we go along as to where you might find yourself being. And the list goes from ten schools to five to three and pretty soon one jumps out based upon what that school offers in terms of how you fit in and the three categories that I talked about.

"I was fortunate in that I had two children who realized that basketball has been my life and I understand about that. While I would never tell them what to do, I always felt I knew the questions to ask. The one thing I would always tell parents who would ask me and didn't know much about the recruiting process is, 'When a college coach comes into your home, before they ask you any questions, you ask them two questions: (1) Are you offering my child a paid forty-eight-hour visit; and (2) if you are and he goes and he says I want to commit right now, does he have a scholarship?' That will cut through the bullshit real quick. Because to get a paid campus visit you have to be one of a select number of kids that they're recruiting. And then if you go and you like that school and you come back and say I want to commit now, if they won't accept your commitment that means you're down their list and there are other people they want to get before they get you. Once you get the answers to those two questions you know exactly where you stand with a college."

What to Look For in a College Coach

Before you know what to look for in your college coach you need to know why the coach is so important. In high school, an outstanding athlete can dominate competition regardless of the coach. In professional sports, because the caliber of athlete is so high across the board, a coach's input, though important, is frequently limited by, or overruled by, the talent—and salaries—of his players. But college is a coach's game because a college coach is, in essence, a coach, a general manager, and a director of player personnel, and not only has an immense amount of control over the way games are played and your role in those games, he/she also has a great deal to say about your collegiate experience off the playing field.

Because coaches are so powerful and important at the collegiate level, it's essential to learn as much as you can about your possible coach. Here are some reasons why.

1   The coach recruits players to fill needs.
2   The coach determines the team's style of play.
3   The coach, in large part, helps set the team's nonleague schedule.
4   The coach runs practices.
5   The coach determines playing time.
6   The coach has to oversee your classroom performance and be in contact with your professors.
7   The coach puts forth an image to the media that reflects upon you and your teammates.

8   The coach helps with summer jobs, alumni contacts, and
        postgraduate (or professional) contacts.
9   You'll spend more time with your coach than with almost
        anyone but your roommate.
10 The success of your team, which will be a direct reflection
        on the quality of the coach and the respect he/she engen-
        ders on campus and in the community, will have a direct
        bearing as to how you are viewed on campus and in your
        community.

So, since your college coach is basically going to be determining
a good portion of your life for four years, as well as laying a foundation
that may influence you many years after that, you want to try to use
some care and common sense when picking who that coach is going
to be. Here are some of the things to look out for.

A Coach Who Cares about You as an Individual

"The main thing, number one, if you're going anywhere to play under
any coach," according to Saudia Roundtree, "is you need to get to
know that coach because if that coach only wants you for your athletic ability then you don't need to go there. Some coaches don't care
about the player as an individual. They only care about their talent.
The reason I chose the University of Georgia was Coach Landers. He
cares about his players on and off the court, not just on the court.
And that was really important to me because I didn't want a coach
who was just going to use me for my basketball talents. If I had a
problem I could go to him. If I needed his help with anything or
needed to talk to him about anything, he was always there. And those
are the types of people that you should look for. Don't just go to a
school because they have a good program. You need to check that
program out. You can get a good education anywhere. But you're going to have to play for this person for years and be happy and if they
don't care about you as a person than there's no sense in you going
there because you're not going to be happy.

"When your coach cares about you on and off the court then
you're going to want to go out and give that person one hundred ten

percent every day in practice because he's a good person and cares about his players."

Roundtree stresses that a student athlete should also take into account the types of players a coach recruits. "You've got to know what type of program you're going into," she says. "You don't want to be with a bunch of players who party all the time. You've got to visit a school and know who's there and know who's going to be there when you get there, and what type of rules the coaches have, because a lot of coaches don't really have rules and let their players do anything."

Before choosing a collegiate coach you should spend quality, one-to-one time with the head coach to determine his or her ability to communicate with you as an individual. Do not take this for granted. Some student athletes are looking for their coaches to be father figures, others are looking to be treated as adults or equals. Not every coach can be all things to all people, so it's important that you either find a coach who fills *your* needs or be confident you will be able to adapt to your coach's needs.

Regardless of individual characteristics, you are going to have to trust your coach. While it may be too much to ask for a coach to be well versed in communicating in the language of a high school student, you must feel that the coach is being honest with you and will treat you fairly. If and when you visit the school, you will probably have a student host—most likely a player on the team—and that host will have been chosen by the coaching staff and probably best represents the coach's philosophies. It's your responsibility to ask other team members how well they relate to the head coach. Here are a few other questions to ask that might give you a better sense of what type of person the coach is.

- *Sense of humor:* Has anyone on the team ever seen the coach laugh?
- *Sense of compassion:* Is the coach helpful if a team member shows up at his or her office with a problem?
- *Mood swings:* How differently does the coach react after a loss than a win?
- *Motivation:* Does the coach get the team ready to play?
- *Laying blame:* What are practices like after tough losses?

- *Sense of unity:* Is there a feeling of togetherness among team members or is the team split into various groups? Are there any divisions along racial lines? Do the upperclassmen get along with the lowerclassmen? Do the players feel the coach plays favorites?

Be wary if players won't answer the tough questions. No matter how good a coach is at the Xs and Os, unless his or her team has overwhelming talent, the ability to communicate and motivate are the most important ingredients for success.

Next, ask the coach, present players, and past players (if available) what the coaching staff, particularly the head coach, does for the players outside of athletics. Is the coach only focused on the sport and only concerned with winning or does he or she understand the importance of

- good academic advising;
- study hall;
- quality summer employment;
- adequate and prompt medical attention;
- alumni interaction?

When you're talking to coaches and players from other schools, try to get an honest idea from them what they think of the coach in question and talk to other athletes whom the coach might have recruited. Camps and clinics are good places to ask around about this.

A Coach with a Solid Academic Record

Most important, find out the coach's record with regard to athletes' graduation rates, because your degree will become your springboard to the real world. Tom McMillen believes the graduation rates issue is so important that when he was in Congress, he worked on legislation that now requires colleges to disclose graduation rates. So be sure to ask. You don't want to wind up at a program that's only graduating 5 percent of its athletes. Either that school is admitting athletes who have no business doing college-level work, or the school is paying no attention to the academics of those students once it admits them. With this in mind, McMillen recommends talking to a couple of former players to find out whether the coach is willing to work with a kid for academic purposes or not. Also, ask the coach for a specific list of influential alums interested in helping student athletes make a smooth transition to life after college.

A Coach Who Will Refine You—Not Remake You

Yes, you're going to want a coach who will take your given abilities and improve them, and those improvements frequently may be the result of making fundamental changes in the way you perform. According to professional golfer Fred Funk, a former collegiate coach at Maryland, it's therefore important to find out from a coach what his or her methods of coaching are. Regardless of the sport, unless your skill level is far below what it should be based on your athletic ability or your method of performing increases the possibility of injury, a coach should try to improve what you've got and not change what you've got.

"Some coaches," Funk says, "have an idea that there's only one way to swing a golf club and you've got to swing like that or you don't play. Some kids are really uncomfortable with that and rightly so. A kid with unorthodox moves can be a good player—there are plenty of them out on tour."

If, however, an area of your performance is particularly weak and inconsistent, you should look for a coach who has had success molding the type of player you want to be with the type of skills you want to acquire.

A Coach with Good Connections

If you have athletic ambition beyond college, inquire about what the coach can do to help you reach the pro ranks and what professional sports contacts the coach has. With a potential pro, a good coach can develop the athlete's individual and team skills and conditioning, and also showcase the athlete in specific game situations. Additionally, a well-connected coach can be very helpful getting a player TV exposure, can contact professional scouts, and can get the player into professional camps for a closer look. If you play at a small school with little exposure, a coach with some connections is almost a necessity if you're to move on to the next level.

One other thing to consider here is how a coach's contacts work in your hometown. Philadelphia native and former La Salle basketball star Craig Conlin says that "whenever I had at-home visits with college coaches my biggest question, which seemed to stump a lot of them, was, 'If I go to your school, chances are I'm probably going to come back here to Philadelphia with your degree. Is there a network here so that I can get a job easily?' Meaning, if I go away to UCLA for four years and take my name away from Philadelphia, how is that going to help me come back here and get a job? My biggest thing was, 'What are you going to do for me after graduation? Is it worth me going away or isn't it?' "

A Coach with Some Stability

Another thing to look for when choosing a coach is the coach's history at the school and how much time remains in his/her contract. That goes for the assistant coaches, too. Ask the coaches their plans for the next four years and judge for yourself whether they're committed to the school or whether they're just using it as a stepping-stone to a better job, and whether the school seems committed to them and their coaching philosophies.

You might think a coach is great, but if his/her name keeps being mentioned for other jobs (check local newspapers), or if there are rumblings in the administration about poor performance, a poor attitude, or unreasonable contract demands (check the campus newspaper and try to speak openly with some academic personnel while on campus), that coach may not be around to see you graduate. Try to get some assurances from the coach that he/she expects to be around awhile. But don't take it personally if the coach later leaves for another job.

A Coach with a Winning Record

The won–lost record should also be considered when comparing coaches. No coach wins every game, but a pattern should be detectable. Find out:

- Does the coach have more winning teams than losers?
- Do his/her teams improve from year to year?

- Do they tend to improve as the season goes on?
- How do they fare when they play against supposedly better competition?
- If he/she has coached in more than one place, is the pattern consistent?

Some coaches are good at building teams, but not maintaining them, and some are good at taking a talented team to the next level. Some win with a particular style of play, some change their style each year to match their talent. Some coaches are great in big-game situations, some freeze on the sidelines. Some coaches win no matter where they are, and some coaches don't win anywhere.

You should be wary of a coach who consistently loses, but don't automatically assume he/she is a bad coach. Tough academic requirements, a small student body, an ugly campus, and poor facilities can affect a team as much as a bad coach.

A Coach with Good Media Relationships

When choosing a coach, you might want to consider how the coach gets along with the media—both local and campus. If you play a low-profile sport, your coach may only interact with reporters from the local or student paper. But if you play a sport with a higher profile, even at a smaller school, your coach will make occasional television appearances, be interviewed on the radio, and be frequently quoted by the press. When you visit campus, check available media sources, try to talk to the school's sports information director about what type of media relationships the coach has, and, if you're very concerned, call the reporter at the daily newspaper who covers the team. It's unorthodox, but perfectly within your bounds.

When checking out the local media about coverage, look to see:

- Do stories seem to be positive or negative?
- Does the coach appear like someone who's in control or like a whining crybaby?
- Does he/she accept responsibility for poor play or is a loss always somebody else's fault?

Be wary of coaches who always sound paranoid. Because coaching is a job with little security, it's common for coaches to look over their shoulders. But keep in mind that it's tough to play for someone who sees conspiracies everywhere. He/she tends to be strung a little tighter than necessary.

Another aspect to consider regarding the coach's relations with the media is what his/her policy is regarding players and the media. Are players allowed to speak to reporters? Are they allowed to be contacted by reporters? On some teams only the captains speak, or only the seniors, or only the upperclassmen. John Thompson, basketball coach at Georgetown University, is famous for the tightfisted way he handles media access to his players. Most student athletes, especially if they're shy or uncomfortable speaking in front of large groups, like the press to be kept away, but if you like the limelight and like to hear yourself talk, ask the coach about his/her policies.

A Coach Who Stays Cool under Fire

When attending a practice and/or a game, you should pay attention to how the coach relates to his/her players in the heat of battle. "A recruit should look at the interaction between a coach and team at a game," coach Ann Sage says. "That will enable the student athlete to see happy players and players who are stressed. The players will tell it like it is."

A Coach Who *Really* Wants You

Lastly, ask the coaches how many players they are recruiting at your position and try to find out how big a priority you are. No matter how much you like a coach, it doesn't do you much good if you don't make the team or don't ever get to play.

On this issue, coach Ann Sage says that "a big recruiting tool is, Yes, you can play here. We need you. You could be a sleeper." But it's important for the student to look at the overall team situation and not just listen to what the coach says. Sage says that the high school athlete should understand that if he/she goes to a large school he/she might be the fifth player off the bench, but that he/she may start at a smaller school and eventually be a better player than the all-star who was recruited ahead of him/her.

"Players can find out from each other what they need to do to make a specific team," Sage says. "That's really important."

How to Prepare for Meeting a Coach

Now that you've got an idea what to look for in a coach, here are a few tips for your sessions together.

1 Bring a notepad and pen.
2 Have your questions ready.
3 Talk to the head coach and assistant coaches individually, but also try to get a sense of how they interact with each other. A good place to do this is at practice, at a team meal, or if the coaches take you to dinner during your visit.
4 Ask the same questions more than once, in different ways if possible, a few hours apart.
5 Do not accept quips or one-liners as answers. If a coach has big reputation, he/she may not want to answer a difficult question and will try to get by on charm alone. It's difficult for any teenager to question the sincerity of an adult—especially one whom you may be trying to get to recruit you—but if a coach laughs off your concerns when he/she is supposedly trying to recruit you, the situation certainly won't get any better once you commit. So if a coach is just cracking jokes instead of answering your questions, politely laugh and later ask for a few minutes of the coach's time—alone. You don't want to embarrass the head coach in front of anyone by continually probing with the same questions, but you also don't want to leave campus without getting answers.

If there's an obvious difference in the responses or a lack of consistency between the coaches, you may have discovered a divided staff. Take it as a warning.

Be prepared to face many different coaches with many different styles. Some coaches are revved-up, enthusiastic salesmen who are also excellent tacticians and swell human beings and others have the same great selling skills but can't coach. Others are serious, low-key, maybe even boring, but can coach their socks off and will provide you with an enriching experience, and still others with the exact same demeanor couldn't coach Dan Marino through a game of Pop Warner football (although that's a case where the coach wouldn't matter).

So try to get to know the coaches who are recruiting you, or whom you are contacting, the best that you can before you make your college choice. And don't make it on coach alone. Weigh the coach's pluses and minuses against those of their various schools, teams, and so on. What you get in terms of education and experience is most important. If you don't play well or get injured, the school situation will begin to seem much more important to you than the coaching situation.

What to Look For in a College

When looking for a college, you'll have many issues to consider, the most important of which is to understand how important this decision is. For the average teenager, picking a college is the biggest decision you've ever made, so it should be given the utmost consideration. This decision, probably more than any other you will make during your teenage years, will have a long-lasting impact on the rest of your life. It is essential that you listen to the advice of those who are close to you and also that you don't jump into any rash decision because you want to get the recruiting process over with. Consider all your options and work hard to improve your options if you're not happy with them.

When you start to think about college choices, and certainly before you start to visit colleges, you should make a list of the elements you wish to consider. Here are some of the basics, with some of the questions you should ask yourself.

Location:
- Do you want to go to college close to home or far away?
- Do you want to go to college in a city, a smaller town, or in a rural area?

Size:
- Do you want to attend a large school or a small school?
- Do you want a liberal arts college or a big university?

Finances:
- Are you assured a scholarship to college?
- Will you only consider schools that offer you a full scholarship? A partial scholarship?
- Should you consider more affordable in-state state colleges?
- If you do not receive a scholarship to college, how much can your family afford to pay?

Academics:
- How important is quality of education to your choice?
- How important is the prestige of the college or university?
- What's more important to your decision, the quality of a school's academics or the quality of a school's sports teams?
- How hard are you willing to work on your academics in college?
- Have you taken all the requirements you need in order to gain admission to the schools of your choice?
- How will the school help you if you wish to continue your education?
- How will the school help you when you enter the job market?
- Is the school strong in areas of study that you believe might be your areas of interest?
- What is the school's faculty-to-student ratio? Compare this to the other schools you are considering. Generally, a lower ratio is considered better, but some top professors only teach large lecture classes.

- Does the school offer a tutoring program?
- What are the graduation rates for student athletes versus the student body as a whole?

Athletics:

- How important is the quality of the sports team recruiting you?
- How important is the reputation of the coach?
- How important is the tradition of the team?
- How important is the quality of the team's conference affiliation?
- How important is winning?
- How important is the chance for playing time? What about immediate playing time?

Social:

- Do the school's living arrangements look as if they will be appealing to you?
- Is it important for you to attend college with friends from high school or your neighborhood?
- Is it important for you to attend college with your present girlfriend or boyfriend?
- Is it important that the school as a whole, and not just the sports teams, have people with backgrounds similar to yours?

If you can honestly answer each of these questions and then match the colleges that you're choosing among to these answers, it should help you narrow your choices down and make a college choice that will be best for you. Just keep in mind one very important thing: Unless you are a lock to have a long and successful career in your sport (and that, unfortunately, is an incredibly small number of you), *you should always weigh your academic issues higher than your athletic issues.*

Here are a few other things to consider, according to Dave Johnson, who deals with thousands of high school and college student athletes every year as director of the Penn Relays.

Johnson says that when you're choosing a college it's important for you to know what it is you want to accomplish and to try to set goals that are realistic, even though your ability to achieve those goals may change, for better or worse, in the coming years. "I know that's very difficult when you're seventeen," Johnson says, "because you're constantly developing and sometimes you can surprise yourself and you find that you're more capable of achieving than you thought you were. Sometimes you wind up setting goals that are way too high.

"It's important to keep in mind that athletes and bodies develop at much different rates. There's always some kid who's great as an eighth or ninth grader and doesn't get much better. And usually it's not because the kid lost interest, but because his body stopped progressing. There are skinny, scrawny kids in ninth grade who don't develop until they're in college. A kid coming out of high school should be most aware of what makes him happy. You're always going to college for the sake of an education—that should be paramount—but there are always kids coming out of high school who think it's important to go to the best school they can get into and they look solely at prestige. They only want to go to the schools that they've heard of and they get into a pool of athletes or students there that is too deep for them. They get in way over their heads and rather than try to continue to compete, they don't even start. That can be true especially if you go to a scholarship school where the athletic program may be limited only to those athletes who are on scholarship or financial aid (partial or otherwise) plus a few walk-ons. A scholarship school probably is not going to have much room for athletes with mediocre ability."

On the academic side, Johnson says, "a high school kid should always look for a place where he can do the academic work. It doesn't help to go to a school where you're going to be swamped. On the other hand, you probably shouldn't worry about that too much, because if you can't do the work—unless you're an absolutely tremendous athlete—the school isn't going to admit you.

"The really exceptional athlete has to be especially wary because so many colleges and coaches and recruiters are willing to bend what is in everyone's best interests. They'll make certain that a kid who barely qualifies for admission can still get in and then they'll hope that the kid can stay afloat academically. The problem with that, though, is that if a kid spends too much time staying eligible, then he's not doing anything well. He's probably not performing that well athletically and that may depress him. If you're over your head, then you should have some second thoughts about a given school.

"The best way to check that," says Johnson, "is to look at some of the college guidebooks that are out there and see what the mean SAT is. On the other hand, and possibly more important, you don't want to get carried away by the thought of an athletic scholarship at some school that's below what you want to achieve academically."

. . . .

By now you may be overwhelmed by the amount of information you've been asked to digest. Don't worry. If you apply only a fraction of the items we've discussed so far you will still be way ahead of your peers making the same decisions you are. The objective here is to make you aware of various areas that you should consider—either consciously or subconsciously—and let your own analysis, instincts, and goals lead you to your decision.

 # Making the Right Choice

Now that you have considered what is and isn't important to your college decision and determined what character traits—in a coach and in a school—will be important to you, you have to start the selection process by compiling a list of the schools you wish to visit. Even if you have dreamed of attending a particular college since you were a kid, it is a good idea to visit a few others. It may even be a good idea to visit another school that you think you're interested in—so that you can compare your impressions with reality and also have some firsthand information about the differences between college campuses, atmospheres, and course offerings.

Getting the Most out of Your Campus Visits

Although you can take an unlimited number of unofficial visits to schools in which you might have some interest, remember that

NCAA regulations allow you only five official visits. It is therefore important to use your visits wisely.

The Unofficial Visit

As a student athlete, you are entitled to make as many "unofficial" visits as you have time and money for. An "unofficial" visit is when you make the plans yourself and pay for it yourself. According to the NCAA, "You can visit a college campus any time at your expense. On such a visit, you may receive three complimentary admissions to a game on that campus and a tour of off-campus practice and competition sites in your sport and other college facilities within 30 miles of the campus."

Many student athletes choose to visit local schools unofficially and save the official visits for faraway trips. However, if you have serious interest in the local school, it's a good idea to make your visit official—it will give you access to a greater number of people, it will show the coach how serious you are, and it will allow you to judge how serious the coach is about you.

If you make an unofficial visit, try to get a sense of the area and the student body. It's difficult to get all the details you need on an unofficial visit, but you can get a "feel" for the place and determine if you then want to make an official visit.

If members of the coaching staff are on campus when you unofficially visit, try to schedule a few minutes to talk, both to get a quick impression of them and to determine if they have any interest in you. As difficult as it may be, you must try to be very objective during these conversations and hear what is being said and not what you want or expect to hear. That said, some coaches will say what they think you want to hear whether they believe it or not. It is important to try to cut through the nonsense so that you don't get strung along by a coach or get trapped in a situation that you've been led to believe will be different than the facts suggest.

An example of this would be when a coach says he/she plans to change his/her style of play if you attend. Coaches are creatures of habit and tend to do what has worked for them in the past. And while some great coaches do change their styles to fit their personnel, most try to shoehorn their personnel into their style. Be wary and beware.

If you ask for an official visit and the coach shows little interest, get the hint. You are probably not in the coach's plans. That same coach, however, may be calling you back in a few months if one of the first-choice recruits has chosen to go elsewhere. At that point you have to weigh how much you want to go to a particular school (knowing you're the coach's second or third option) versus loyalty to the coaches who have been recruiting you all along. It's up to you. But keep in mind that if the coach didn't actively recruit you until the end, he/she's probably already recruiting somebody to replace you.

"I don't want to go there if they don't want me" is a good philosophy to have, says Penn Relays director Dave Johnson. "You may want to go someplace but if they aren't head over heels wanting you then that may not be where you ought to be going. You want to go where you're wanted. That's sometimes a tough lesson to learn—that rejection can be for your own good. It's something we all learn eventually."

When planning your "unofficial" visits, try to check out as many schools as you can over the summer between your junior and senior years, with either parents, guardians, relatives, or coaches. If time and finances permit, take a driving vacation with your family and stop at colleges along the way. Another good time to visit schools is when you have a break from classes—but keep in mind that the college will probably also be out of session then, so you may not get an accurate picture of what the campus is like.

The Official Visit

An official visit is one sanctioned by and paid for by a university that is recruiting you. If a coach invites you to make a visit official, you know, at the very least, that the coach has some interest in you as a student athlete, and has some interest in your possibly playing for him/her the following season. How much the coach wants you to attend his/her school remains to be seen, but that's one of the key things you hope to learn from your visit.

Since NCAA rules allow you only five "official" visits, you need to use them wisely. Therefore, before you make any official visits you should do research on the coach, the team, and the school. Check out college guides at a bookstore or your high school library to find out what the school's academic standards are like, what campus social life is like, and what the average student is like. Then you should try to find some magazine articles or newspaper stories—at the library or on the Internet—about the coach and the team. Some questions you should try to answer include:

- Does this school (its location, reputation and academic programs) sound like a place where you would be comfortable?
- Does the school offer courses in the subjects you're interested in?
- Are your grades comparable to those of other students and/or other athletes?

For team sports, questions you want answered should include:

- What style does the team play?
- Does the coach play a lot of players, or a few?
- Has there been any recent turmoil on the team?
- How many people come to see the team play? How does that number (be it large or small) compare to other teams in that same sport and especially other teams in that school's league?
- What kind of media coverage do the school's teams get? Obviously, most college sports and most college teams are not on ESPN, but what kind of coverage do the teams get in the local media and in the campus newspaper?

Knowing the answers to these questions in advance will make your campus visit much more productive and informative because you will be able to focus in on the areas that you aren't sure about.

The "official" visit is important because it should (if handled properly) give you an opportunity to interact with a cross section of athletes, coaches, faculty members, administrators, and, frequently, alumni. It should provide you with an excellent tour of the campus and the surrounding area and also give you a sense of campus life. If all goes well (from the coach's point of view), you will get a completely biased, rose-colored picture of the school, making it seem more like Disneyland than college. If the coach wants you, he or she will plan a picture-perfect weekend for you (and if they can make the weather 75 degrees and sunny they'll do that, too). So it's important to pay attention not only to what people are saying to you but what they're *not* saying to you, and not only to what they're showing you but what they're *not* showing you.

The coach will generally have you hosted by an athlete who's both very happy and very committed to the coach's agenda. That's fine. The team may be successful, the coach may be well-liked, and there may be harmony among the players. But sometimes there are troubles in paradise and it's a good idea, while visiting the campus, to try to talk to a few student athletes who aren't on the "approved" list.

If possible, search out a player who may be having academic troubles, may be looking to transfer, or who may have quit the team. It's amazing and unfortunate how many times similar players make the same mistakes simply because they do not open their eyes to the true situation at the school they're interested in. While you visit, get a sense of who plays and who doesn't and try to honestly judge where your style and level of ability fit in. And if you really want and expect to play, talk to some of the players who are warming the bench and find out what their thoughts were when they chose the school and what promises they were made by the coaches.

Craig Conlin says, "To find out coaching-wise what would be a good match, I found the best thing I could do was ask the players on the team, because usually when you go away to visit schools they pair you up with a player or two on the team and they take you around and do the usual things and then at night you stay with them in their dorm room or apartment and that's a good chance to ask, 'What's the deal here?' The coaches are always going to paint a rosy picture. You need to ask the players to give you the truth and then you really have to cut through it. Some guys will tell you, 'You know, it's not all it's cracked up to be.' Usually you can get a gut feeling on that too."

If you're African-American, or a member of any minority group, spend some time with the white student athletes to see not only how you fit in but whether they have any interest in your fitting in. It's the same if you're white—don't spend your entire campus visit hanging with members of some all-white fraternity or sorority. Sports teams are frequently the most racially integrated and racially harmonious of all social groups on campus, but it's never bad to know if they're not.

Although you want your visit to be fun, the visit is, in a sense, your first business trip—the coach and players are trying to determine whether they want to start a working relationship with you and you want to determine whether you want to start a working relationship with them. A sad part of recruiting student athletes is that students tend to spend more time buying their first car than on choosing their college. During your campus visits it's important that you check the steering, enjoy the look and color, and, by all means, kick the tires. Your college career will probably last longer than your first car—and it will certainly pay off more down the road.

Carry a pad, pencil, and a prepared list of questions with you that you can refer to when necessary (you also may want to carry a small tape recorder and record your impressions so you can refer to them later). Questions to ask the coach and/or players may include:

1   What kind of tutoring services are available?
2   What percentage of the players graduate?
3   What types of options are there for living arrangements?
4   How much help is available for picking courses?
5   How much classwork do players miss due to away-game travel?
6   What role does the coach see for you—short term and long term?
7   How many other student athletes is the coach recruiting at your position (or in your event)?
8   If you commit, will the coach bring in anyone else at your position (or in your event)?
9   What does the coach think your strengths and weaknesses are?
10 Does the coach recruit junior college players?
11 Does the coach start (or offer significant playing time to) freshmen?

12 What aspects of your game (technique, etc.) should you work on over the summer?

13 Would the coach provide you with a drill sheet to develop your skills?

14 What time does the coach generally schedule practices or workouts?

15 What is the coach's general policy regarding discipline?

Also ask the coach a few personal questions which might catch him/her off guard:

16 What types of players are your favorites? Are you that type of player?

17 If the coach played in college, ask: What type of player were you? (Coaches frequently look for players with qualities they had. Are you that type of player?)

18 If the coach is married, ask: What does your wife/husband think of your profession?

Coaching college sports (especially at the higher levels) is a high-stress job with little security. Coaches can be insecure, edgy, and very competitive. By asking a few personal questions you might be able to see another side of the coach—a side separate from the whistle-blowing, screaming maniac that you might see in practice or at games. Getting a sense of whether you like the coach as a person may help you with your final decision.

If you get the chance, also ask as many of these questions as possible of the assistant coaches and see if there are any (or many) contradictions. When a staff of coaches gives you different answers, it could signal some internal dissension and may be something to consider.

Two final items to discuss with the coach:

1 If a professional career is an option in your sport and you have aspirations in that direction, ask the coach what he/she can do to help make that dream come true.

2 If a career in professional sports is not a realistic goal (and for almost everyone, it isn't), ask the coach what he/she can do to help you get a job when you graduate.

What to Look For When Talking to a Coach

You can't pick your relatives, but you can pick your college coach. By paying attention to a few physical and behavioral signals, you can help to avoid a bad choice.

● *Look for eye contact.* Eye contact and a firm handshake are the first indicators of what type of person you're dealing with and will give you an idea if the coach is a confident person. The same is true for you—if you give the coach a weak handshake and avoid making eye contact the coach may think you lack the confidence and inner security to compete at the level he/she is recruiting you for.

● *Look at body language.* Does the coach's posture indicate a willingness and interest in being with you? Is he/she enthusiastic or just going through the motions? Posture says a lot about a person, so be conscious of your own when talking to the coaches and players. You, too, want to come across as mature and confident.

● *Is the coach a fast talker?* Do you sense rapport with the coach? Does he/she seem excitable or bored? Worn out or strung out? Most important, does the coach speak a language that you intuitively understand or is he/she on a different wavelength?

● *Is the coach patient?* Does the coach seem interested in your answers? Bored by your questions? Easily distracted? This is the time when the coach is trying to make a good impression, so if you don't click now, don't expect your relationship to blossom into some buddy-buddy thing later. And that may be just as well. Your coach is not someone with whom you have to want to pal around, go to the movies, study, or play video games.

Remember: The coach is the coach—not your best friend.

By asking the coach a number of prepared questions, you demonstrate that this is not a decision you are taking lightly, and you also get a chance to see how the coach communicates. Communication is often a key factor in coaching—and not only how the coach communicates with recruits and players, but also how the coach communicates with his/her assistant coaches. Ask the assistant coaches (in sports in which there are assistant coaches) how they get along with the head coach.

- Are their suggestions taken?
- Do they get to lead practices?

You don't want to be heavily recruited by an assistant coach only to find out the head coach is seriously interested in someone else.

During your campus visits, make sure you allocate time for visiting with academic advisers and administrators. If the coach hasn't set up these appointments, ask him/her to do that (although not setting up these appointments should give you a sense of how important the coach rates academics). Also, set aside time to meet with a few professors (preferably in a field of study in which you're interested). Minority students should always try to meet with a tenured minority professor (tenure guarantees a professor a job for life)—first to see if there is any type of minority presence in the faculty, and, second, to see how minority athletes are viewed by the campus community. A tenured professor will generally give you straight answers and could prove to be a tremendous resource for you should you attend that school.

Remember: It is always a good idea to visit a school at least once before committing to the school. You are deciding to spend four very important years of your life there, and as the old Holiday Inn advertisement once said: "The best surprise is no surprise." If time and money permit, it is also a good idea to try to visit the school again unofficially—talk to students, hang around, try to get a feel for the place—to see how much of the "official" sales pitch was true.

Narrowing Down Your College Choices

Once you have done your research, talked to the coaches who are recruiting you, and made your campus visits, it is time to narrow down your choices. Remember, the earlier you make your college choice the less pressure (and more fun) you will have your senior year in high school.

A student athlete should make his or her choice the way any prospective college student would, only the student athlete has a few more factors—the athletic factors—to consider.

Making a Checklist

Take all of the colleges you are considering and write each school's name at the top of its own piece of paper. Then fold each piece of paper in half. Write "Academics" on one half and "Athletics" on the other half.

Academics

Here are some of the questions to answer on the "Academics" half. Give each school a numerical rating for each question to give you a quick overview of the competition. If you are choosing between five schools, for instance, rate the schools 1 to 5 on each question and then tally up the results.

1 *How does the school rate academically compared to your other possible choices?* No college rating guide is completely objective, so take three or four different guides and average how your schools are rated with regard to their academic reputations, the size and quality of their faculty, the depth and breadth of their course offerings, and the average scores of their incoming students. This will give you an idea of how others see the list of schools you are choosing from.

2 *Which school's diploma will mean the most regarding future job opportunities?* College guides can again be helpful here but you can also call the coaches and admissions offices for information about the average starting salaries of recent graduates and lists of prominent alumni whom you might be able to contact.

3 *Which of the schools has the most to offer in the area you wish to study?* Get copies of each school's course guide and compare course offerings for quantity and quality. Determine how the course offerings are spread out over requirements, and beginning and advanced courses. Does the school offer graduate courses that you can take as an undergraduate? Check out where the various professors have studied and how much they have published. Ask admissions

personnel what percentage of classes are taught by full professors and what percentage by teaching assistants.

4 *What is the average classroom size?* This information should be available from the admissions office. Keep in mind that introductory survey classes will often be in large lecture halls (and that is not always a bad thing).

5 *Which school seems to have the best academic support for athletes?* Talk to coaches, admissions officers, faculty members, and academic advisers to determine the type of help you will get and the type of help they feel you will need. Also, when you visit the campus, talk to student athletes about the quality and availability of tutoring.

6 *What percentage of athletes in your sport graduate?* This information should be available from the coach, the athletic department, the admissions office, or the alumni relations office. If it isn't, check with the league office or the NCAA, or ask your local newspaper to do a search for you on graduation rates.

7 *Did you feel comfortable on campus during your visit?* Did the players make you feel welcome? Did the coaches? Did you feel as if you would be comfortable talking to the coaches about any personal problems? Did the campus seem like the type of place in which you would like to live? How was the surrounding environment or neighborhood? What about the campus social life?

8 *Can you do the classwork?* Don't kid yourself on this issue. The best college choice will almost always be the one that challenges your mind and your athletic ability to the highest realistically achievable degree, but aiming too high could be as destructive as aiming too low will be unfulfilling. You are setting up a foundation for the rest of your life with this choice and you don't want to waste these all-important years struggling—or coasting.

"When I was applying to colleges," says Olympic fencer Peter Cox, "I didn't know what I wanted to major in. I didn't even know anything about Penn State except that it had a very diverse selection of majors and obviously I was going to school to [find a career] and I just wanted to be well-rounded. So the school offered a lot of selections as far as a good liberal arts education, so that's what I looked for. I was thinking about medicine back then—so I was also looking at Ivy schools like Penn—but I didn't know if I could actually hack it academically at Penn *and* reach the goals I wanted to in fencing.

"Maybe I could have gone to a better college at the time I was coming out of high school, but at the time I had trouble with multiple-choice tests and I couldn't score over twelve hundred on the SATs. The Penn coach said he might be able to get me in, but I was trying to be honest with myself and I was afraid that I might go there and drop out or not be able to help the school the way they wanted me to. At Penn State I knew I could get the attention that I needed and also learn to take big tests because it's a larger school. Being honest with yourself lets you know where you stand and it gives you a strong base no matter what people tell you."

The choice turned out to be a good one for Cox. He made it to the Olympics and is now a doctor of chiropractic medicine.

Athletics

On the "Athletics" side of each paper, try to answer these questions.

1 *How does the team rate compared to your other possible choices?* It's impossible to judge how a team will fare in the future, but past performance is generally a reasonable indicator. If you're considering two traditional Division I powers there probably isn't that much difference between the two, but if you're considering a mid-level Division I program and a high-level Division II program, there could be a number of differences. Check how the teams have performed over the past few years. Check the average attendance at home and away games. Have the teams recently competed in an NCAA tournament? Are any of the teams rebuilding? Do the teams have any longtime winning tradition, a tradition of alumni support, or a history of sending athletes to the professional level if a professional level exists in your sport?

2 *How does the coach rate?* Compare how each of the coaches have done at the schools you are considering and also check to see how they've done at schools they might have been at previously. Do they have a history of winning? Of graduating their players?

Of helping their players succeed after graduation? When you visit the campus, talk to current players about the coach and coaching staff to determine how the coaches get along with their players.

3 *Is there stability in the program?* Some programs have the same coach for decades and never experience a hint of scandal. Other programs change coaches as frequently as athletes change their socks. Take note of the situation at the schools you're considering and factor stability into your decision. Keep your ears open for any rumors of dissension or dismissal. You don't want to have to adjust to a new coach while you're still adjusting to what is already a new situation. Also, make note of the stability *on* the team. Do student athletes stay for four years? Has the team been hit by a rash of transfers, defections, or academic suspensions?

4 *Will you feel comfortable with the style of play?* This is another area where you shouldn't kid yourself. Coaches have certain styles and tend not to change them. A coach might tell you that he/she's going to change in order to suit your talents—especially if the coach really wants you—but take these promises with a grain of salt. The coach is probably saying the same thing to all his recruits. When you talk to potential teammates, try to get a sense of what practices are like, what off-season sessions are like, what strategy sessions are like, and what games/meets are like. Determine whether you will be comfortable in such a system.

5 *Will you play right away?* If a coach would, shall we say, fib about style of play, wait until you ask about playing time. If the coach has done his/her homework, you're going to hear whatever you want to hear. If you're a highly touted recruit who expects to play immediately, that's what you're going to be told. If you're a lesser recruit who expects to be brought along slowly, that's what you're going to be told. First decide how important immediate playing time—or any playing time—is to you and then see how your choices will fit in. The truth is, nobody really knows how much you will play in a coming season because your playing time is going to be determined by both your improvement over the coming months and the improvement of your future teammates. When you're comparing your schools, check their team's rosters and determine how many players they have at your position and what years they are. When you visit a campus, ask your possible teammates what their expectations for the coming seasons are. And certainly ask the coaches who else they are recruiting at your position and how many of these recruits they hope to bring in.

6 *Is the level of competition a good fit for your abilities?* Are you going to be in over your head or are you going to be at a level where you can improve and excel? If you are choosing between teams in different conferences or divisions, try to determine the overall level of play and how you would fit in. Could you play a significant role for other teams in the league? Are you being recruited by comparable teams? Shooting too high is okay if you're prepared to struggle. Don't shoot too low.

7 *If you don't develop immediately, will you be recruited right over?* No coach is going to say yes to that question, so don't even ask it. The way you find out the answer is to ask players on the team, especially any who might be disgruntled, and check playing time over the past few years.

8 *Does the team have a history of winning?* It's not an accident that some teams are always near the top of their respective conferences. They frequently have the best coaches, the best facilities, and the most supportive alumni base. At the lower levels of college competition, sometimes what separates the winners from the losers is the schools' commitment to winning. Do they take sports seriously? Do they support their teams?

9 *How important is winning?* If you have to make choice between playing a little for a powerhouse or playing a lot for a mediocre team, be ready with your answer. If you come from a winning high school tradition, are you going to be able to take not winning? Do you have enough confidence in the coach and your own abilities that you may be able to turn a team into a winner?

10 *Did you feel comfortable with your potential teammates during your visit to campus?* These are people that you are going to practice with, study with, travel with, room with, and compete with—do you feel like you can be a part of their team? Did you notice any

cliques or factions dividing the players? Did you get a sense of cama-
raderie and support among the players?

11 *How much media exposure will you get?* Depending on
your sport, the size of your school, and the size of its location, you
should be able to get a sense of the possible media attention. When
you're in town for a visit, read the local papers and watch the local
news to see if college athletics gets much coverage. In some areas, a
major university is the equivalent of a professional franchise and even
the so-called minor sports are widely supported by the community.
Smaller colleges may not rack up the same large attendance figures,
and you may travel by bus instead of private chartered jet, but there
might be a strong interest from the local media and area residents.

12 *Is media exposure important to you?* Since it's become so
popular to blame the media for just about everything, media attention may not be important to you. You may not want the pressure of
being closely watched and having your actions reported in print and
on television. Bad press can go a long way to ruining a promising career and putting you and your teammates under an unfair magnifying
glass that makes it hard for you to perform to the best of your abilities. However, good press and TV exposure can give you a springboard to a career in professional athletics or offer you exposure to potential employers when your college career is over.

13 *Is media exposure realistic for you (given your sport or your
ability)?* Let's face it, football players get more coverage than
fencers, and football players at Notre Dame get more attention than
football players at Swarthmore. That's just the way it is. If you play a
sport that doesn't get any media coverage anywhere, you can't hold
that against the school. So take a realistic look at the potential for media exposure and keep in mind that no matter what you play or where
you play, if you're good enough you can make it to the next level.

Other Factors to Consider as You Narrow Down Your Choices

In addition to the academic and athletic issues on your checklist,
there are other, more subjective, criteria you need to weigh.

- *The school's location.* Will you be too far from home? Will you be too close to home? Will your parents/guardians, relatives, and friends be able to see you play? Is that important to you? Will the adjustment from a big city to a small town (or vice versa) be too great?

- *The school's cost.* If you are not going to get a full scholarship offer, or if you are choosing to go to a school that does not offer athletic scholarships, how much can your family afford? How much will vacation travel home add to the cost? Will the quality of the education outweigh the cost?

- *The school's extracurricular activities.* How will your quality of life be during those rare periods when you are not practicing or studying? Are there enough activities on campus to fill your time, or will you need to travel off campus? Do you feel as if you would be a good fit in the student body? Will the campus community broaden your perspective and introduce you to different types of people?

- *The school's fraternity/sorority scene.* On some campuses, the athletes help define Greek life; on others, the Greek scene is merely another living option. First you should find out how important Greek life is at the schools you're considering, then you have to decide if that matters.

- *The athletes' living conditions.* Are athletes an integral part of the campus community, campus celebrities, or a sideshow? Do athletes live apart from or with the general student body? You need to guess at the type of living arrangement in which you will feel most comfortable and factor that into your decision.

- *The relationship between athletes and alumni.* Does your team have strong alumni support? Are there networking channels in place for you to seek career advice or employment? Are boosters too active and liable to cost you and your team your NCAA standing?

- *The school's policies regarding your financial package should you be injured or academically ineligible or decide to give up your sport.* Different leagues and different schools have different policies regarding these matters; you should talk to a coach and a financial aid officer about them before making your decision.

● *The school's and the league's transfer policies.* If you determine that you have made a bad choice and seek a transfer, are there
any policies that will limit your options or eligibility?

● *What your advisers say.* When making a decision as important, as where to go to college, doses of reality and maturity are
important, so you should seek advice from as many adults as you
can—including trusted teachers, guidance counselors, recent alums,
relatives, guardians, and, of course, parents.

Since your parents almost always have your best interests at
heart (even if you may not always think so)—and since, in the case of
college, they're probably footing the bill—you cannot dismiss their
advice and recommendations. Listen carefully to their opinions and
talk out your differences. It is important for your parents (or
guardians) to understand your concerns, just as it is important for you
to understand theirs.

When Olympic swimmer Cristina Teuscher, from one of New
York's northern suburbs, was making her college choice, she had an
extra factor to figure in—her personal coach. Like many world-class
caliber athletes in individualized sports (swimming, golf, tennis, fencing, gymnastics, etc.), Teuscher had been training with Coach John
Collins for years, and wasn't sure if she wanted to leave the coach
who had prepared her for the Olympics in favor of a new collegiate
coach.

"My choices came down to Stanford, USC, SMU, and Columbia," Teuscher says. "I visited Michigan, Florida, and Princeton as
well, but I decided not to apply to those schools. I looked at my priorities and my family is most important to me and I wanted to be close
to them and swimming was at the top, so I decided to go to Columbia
so I could be close to Coach Collins and continue to swim with him.
That's what kept me here. I think it's really important to list your *real*
priorities. I just didn't take into account the little things like the
weather and the number of people in the school, but if you really like
the people and you can really see yourself there. I'm one of those
people that believes that you can feel it when you get to a school. You
can really feel if you belong there or not.

"I think the most important thing for a student is that they have to like the school as well as they like the athletic aspect of it. You have to think of it as if something happened to you and you would never be able to do your sport in your life—say I would never be able to swim again—would I still enjoy being at this school. And then you really have to decide what you're looking for—how big you want the school, whether you think the coach will add to your success, and whether you think you can trust the coach."

Rhodes scholar Tom McMillen agrees. "At any point in time, this whole thing can come tumbling down. You could break a leg or be a hit by a car. And you have to realize that your best insurance policy is your education, and if you don't realize that then you're being very foolhardy. The fact is that most kids don't make it and you should not put your eyes on something where the odds are stacked against you. I think you've got to keep your priorities."

Don't Make Your Decision Alone

Open communications are very important. Mom may want you to be a brain surgeon and Dad may want you to be a linebacker for the Dallas Cowboys, but in reality you're only a C+ student who is 5'10" and weighs 180 pounds. Know your limitations and discuss them openly and honestly. "It's sometimes very difficult to be honest in front of your parents," Dave Johnson acknowledges. "It's hard to tell your parents that you don't like to be pushed all the time. But when you get to college you're not going to have your parents sitting over you. You're going to have to do all the work. And you've got to find a situation where either the peer group will pull you along academically or you're pushing yourself. You've got to find what your own motivation is in the same way that's true of athletics."

But if you pick the right college and really apply yourself you can still make Mom proud and be that brain surgeon. Dad, however, may just have to be content to watch you play at a level a few notches below the NFL. "Every school in the country," says Johnson, "no matter how high or how low on the academic scale, has very good students and you can succeed at any school—but you can also fail at any school. It will entirely come down to your own motivation."

As for economics, parents and guardians also have to factor what they can reasonably afford to pay into your decision and may try to pressure you into a choice (community college, city school, or state school) that is more affordable. Or you may have family obligations that make it impossible for you to move far away. When these options need to be considered, your goal is to make the best compromise choice—choosing the school that offers the most long-term benefits for you and your family. Yes, you might have to sacrifice something either in academics or athletics, but sacrifice is a part of growing up. The key is to make your sacrifices and compromises wisely and not jump into rash decisions you will later regret. Besides, no matter where you go to college, if you apply yourself you will succeed.

The Final Cut

Once you have thought about all the areas mentioned above and compared the various schools you are considering, you have to pare down your list to a manageable number of two or three schools. In making your short list, you should decide all of your big issues so that the remaining schools are somewhat similar, although it's not a bad idea for one of them to be something of an academic stretch for you and one of them (possibly the same one) to be something of an athletic stretch. If, however, you're down to three schools and one of them is a gigantic state university in an industrial center, one of them is a small liberal arts college in the mountains, and one of them is a religious school, you're going to have a terrible time making your final decision because you're going to have to recompare every school on every issue. Get the big issues out of the way (type of school, location of school, quality of play, quality of academics), and then you can concentrate on the subtle differences between the schools and ask pointed questions of the coaches and administrators.

Should a school start recruiting you late in the process, you and your advisers have to decide if you're mentally ready to start factoring in new data and if you want to let another contender in. Why is this school recruiting you so late? Did a player get injured? Did their top recruits decide to go somewhere else? Or did they just find out about you? You owe some loyalty to the coaches who have been recruiting you all along to give them an edge, but ultimately it's your future. And if your dream school comes in late, no matter what the reason, you have to give the school some attention if you honestly believe they are being straight with you. Just make sure that you do not turn your back on a coach who really wants you and is committed to your game in favor of a coach who sees you as a fill-in to warm the bench, bring up the grade point average of the recruits he/she really wants, or because you're a hometown prospect who the coach feels he/she needs to recruit in order to save face and gain publicity in the local community.

If a coach plays hardball with you, demanding a decision by a certain date, explain your reservations about a quick decision to the coach and do your best to stall. If the coach really wants you, he/she will understand. In the big-revenue sports, however, where signing top recruits is essential if the coach is to keep his/her high-paying job, the coach may want you but still pressure you because if you don't commit quickly and then decide to go somewhere else, his/her second choice might also be gone by then. Recruiting is a cutthroat business, and because it is so high pressure many young people are pressured into making bad choices. Don't be one of them.

Moving Up to the Next Level: How to Spend Your Summer Vacation

O nce you graduate from college and enter the workforce, summer is a lot like the rest of the year, but warmer. But while you're still in school, summer is a time to unwind—to have fun, maybe get a summer job, and also recharge your energies for the school year ahead. Summer is also a time to focus on improving yourself and there's no summer more important than the one between your senior year of high school and your freshman year of college. You must look at the 8–10 week summer vacation period as a season independent of (yet related to) your regular season of academics and athletics.

There are three basic areas to concentrate on if you want to hit college ready to roll: academics, athletics, and social skills.

Academics

The scholarship athlete especially should concentrate on academics, as the granting of an athletic scholarship implies that you have the basic athletic tools needed to compete at the collegiate level. If you are also an honor student in an excellent high school with a number of AP credits already on your transcript, you are probably well on your way to being adjusted for college-level classwork. But since most of you are not carrying a 4.0 GPA, it is highly recommended that you attend a prefreshman program at your college of choice—almost all schools now offer them.

If attending this program is impossible (it's not offered, it costs too much, you can't get out of your summer job, etc.), then you should try to spend at least one session in summer school, learning to prepare for college-type courses such as calculus, economics, statistics, English composition, and/or other courses in which you might feel behind or troubled. How you fare in these prerequisite courses will determine how easy or difficult your transition to college work will be, and they also may also help you determine a field of study. As in athletics, you want to play to your strengths and interests—not to your weaknesses.

Since you will be required to balance academics with athletics once the school year begins, why not get a head start during your summer vacation? Map out a schedule combining class time, training time, study time, job time, social time, and game time. Then, after the Fourth of July, start an intensive 6–8 week program incorporating summer school, competition or league play, and individual development.

One of your biggest transitions to college will be dealing with the academic demands of college professors and college courses, so you should plan accordingly. Ask your high school coach, academic adviser, favorite teacher, or parent for creative ways to prepare for the rigors of college.

Your high school coach should be able to give you the names of specific sports camps that also offer sessions on academic preparation.

Your academic adviser should be able to give you the names of specific books or prep courses.

Your teacher should be able to explain how classroom demands (especially in his/her subject) will change in college and give you an idea as to what you should expect. A good teacher should also be able to analyze your performance (not just from a grade standpoint but from your work level and achievement standpoint) and let you know in what areas you need to improve.

Your parent or guardian should be able to provide you with the support needed (and moral support is frequently as important as financial support) to attend summer programs, camps, prefreshman programs, and so on.

In your prefreshman summer school academic program, it is very important to challenge yourself beyond that of the basic high school curriculum. If you have a strong foundation of basic studies and you're not struggling just to stay afloat, do not shy away from the more demanding disciplines of study such as computer science, engineering, accounting, physics, chemistry, and so on. This is a good time to broaden your areas of interest and learn of new fields of study in which you might be interested. This summer school philosophy should stay with you throughout college as you use the summer not just to make up lost ground but to expand your intellectual horizons.

Book smarts and coursework, however, are only two of the tools that will help you in college. You will also need to improve specific *learning skills*. This is a big list, but any one of the items listed below can help to give you an edge.

Listening

The more you can understand in class, the more knowledge you have to call on for classroom answers or exams. Most of us hear, but few of us listen. Listening is more than hearing—it's hearing and comprehending and analyzing and synthesizing and storing for further use.

A good way to improve your listening skills is to get a few audiobooks from either a bookstore or the local library. Listen to the tapes for a half hour, maybe even take notes as if you were listening to a professor's lecture. After a half hour, stop the tape and try to write down as much as you can recall. This will force you to pay attention to what is being said.

Note Taking

The better your notes, the quicker you'll be able to relearn new information. The key to good note taking is not writing down everything that is said (then you would just have to read it all back), but writing down the important things that are said. You will have a much better sense of what's important if you have a basic understanding of the topic and come to class prepared. If you are not prepared, everything will seem new and mysterious to you and you may overestimate its importance.

Study Habits

The better you concentrate when you study, the more efficient you'll be and the more time you'll have for other things. It's common for college students to brag about how much they study or how much time they spend in the library, but much of that time (except among the really smart students) is wasted—they're looking around, listening to music, letting their minds wander, et cetera. The key to good studying is good concentration, the ability to tune out distractions and focus.

Classroom Participation and Public Speaking

If you're comfortable speaking in front of people, you will be more likely to participate in class. Classroom participation can offer a huge boost to a student athlete because it helps disprove a stereotype: By joining in discussions and answering questions you show your classmates (and more important, the professor) that you know what's going on—and that you care. Just as coaches like to see effort, professors like to see effort. The harder you try, the more forgiving the professor might be if you need help down the road.

Although most of you will not be interviewed on television, most of you who play sports at the collegiate level will at some time have to speak publicly—either to a reporter from the school newspaper or a local paper, to a potential recruit looking to join your team, to a banquet audience, or to a prominent alum looking to offer you a job. Confidence in public speaking is one of the toughest skills to master, but it comes from confidence in having a large vocabulary, being well read in a variety of topics, knowing proper sentence structure, and feeling comfortable with yourself and who you are. By coming across as a thoughtful student athlete with a command of the language, you will again break an unfair stereotype, be more successful at networking, and also become an athlete more likely to be sought out by the media. People like to talk to people who have something to say.

Reading and Writing

Everyone who goes to college (except for a few scandalous cases that later make the newspapers) believes that he/she knows how to read and write. But reading and writing at a level that can improve your collegiate experience is a completely different ball game. Think in terms of a race. If it takes you two minutes to read and comprehend a page of text and it takes your roommate one minute to read and understand the same page, how far ahead will your roommate be at the end of a 300-page book? He/she will be out having fun while you're back in the dorm room desperately cramming.

"At this age a lot of kids really don't want to read," says high school coach Craig Conlin. But in terms of helping you academically, he adds, "something as simple as reading is tremendous."

If it takes you a few hours to organize your thoughts and then six more hours to write a six-page paper, think how much more efficient you would be (and how much more time you could put into making that paper great) if you could handle the actual writing in three hours.

One of the biggest advantages you can bring to the college classroom is the ability to read quickly and write in coherent, grammatically correct sentences. A nicely typed paper, with all the words spelled correctly, will score you points and will cover up possible omissions in your information content. When a professor (or teaching assistant) has to read 50 papers on the same topic, getting through the papers can be an ordeal. Making your paper a pleasure to read will be a big asset.

Over the summer, you should therefore try to read as much as possible and also practice writing and word processing—perhaps take a speed-reading course or a typing course. The amount of time you spend improving these skills now will save you countless hours down the road.

Computer and Research Skills

Good research skills are important because they will help you to find new sources to draw information from—sources which may explain your course material better than your professor or your textbook. They will also improve your ability to write papers, because you'll be able to find new and different information that your lazier classmates may not uncover.

Good researchers tend to be very clever because they find sources outside the normal channels. And they find them faster. When time management is essential, every second you can save is a second for you to improve in some other area, to relax, or to sleep. An ability to work in a library, to find reference materials, to use microfilms will help immeasurably. Reference librarians will also do whatever they can to help you. That's their job, and most of them are very good at it. But when seeking help from a librarian, be polite, have your questions ready, and have an idea what you're looking to find. You will be amazed how much help you might be able to get and how many new ideas a good reference librarian might give you.

Many libraries, especially college libraries, now have an incredible amount of reference material available for computer searches. With the World Wide Web, Internet newsgroups, Gopher archival sites, CD-ROMs, and online services like America Online, CompuServe, Prodigy, and more, there is an unlimited amount of information at your fingertips. Knowing basic computer skills and how to access this information will be a key to success.

In addition, virtually all colleges provide computer resource centers and even computers for those of you who don't yet have one of your own. Knowing how to use a word-processing program will be very helpful when you have a paper to write. Other programs geared toward math or science could also be tremendously helpful.

Ask specific teachers, professors, or advisers if there are any programs or applications they recommend. Many of them will be available as free shareware or at very reduced prices from your college bookstore.

Rest and Relaxation

Like reading and writing, everyone thinks they know how to rest and relax. Not so. Rest and relaxation are different, and your mind and body have to know how to do both. Resting has to do with replenishing your physical and mental well-being.

Resting *is not* partying. A party may relax you but it doesn't let your body rest.

Resting *is not* shooting the breeze with your roommate until four in the morning. Talking all hours may ease your mind but it doesn't ease your fatigue.

Where resting and relaxing are one is in cooling down, recharging, and letting go of physical and mental stress. Taking an afternoon nap, a hot shower, listening to quiet music, meditating, or lying out on the grass on a nice sunny day can be both resting and relaxing.

In college, you are going to be putting your mind and body through more stress than they have ever undergone. You will have to find time to unwind or you will overload your circuits. You will hit the wall. Schedule some time every day as your quiet time. Rest.

Where relaxation is different from rest pertains to how you respond to pressure. When you go into a big game, are you relaxed? How about a big test? Many students say they freeze up when they have to take the SATs but are completely calm when an entire cheering section is shouting their names. Relaxation has to do with your comfort zone. Where do you feel at home? What situations produce anxiety? For student athletes, a key to success in the classroom is converting the relaxation you feel during athletic competition into relaxation you'll feel during classroom competition (tests, etc.). Don't let stress negate all of your good studying. Learn coping techniques, see a therapist, talk to your coach. The key is to be honest. No one wants to see you struggle. Your college will provide you with help.

Athletics

It doesn't matter how hard your practices were in high school—they will be harder in college. So summer is a good time to prepare your body for what awaits you in the fall. It's important to remember that just because you were a standout high school athlete does not mean you will immediately, or ever, become a standout collegian. Your size and body type are going to have an effect on how great you can become. However, if you prepare yourself and develop a consistent work ethic, you can help maximize your chances.

The best way to do this is to get a workout schedule from your soon-to-be college coach. Also find out if there are any leagues or meets in which you should be competing. Then, if possible, find yourself a workout partner—either a friend from high school or a college athlete who lives nearby. This way you'll have someone to go to the gym with, someone to compete against, and someone to make you feel guilty if you start to slack off.

There are five important areas in which college athletics will challenge your mind and body.

1 *Cardiovascular output.* The more efficient a muscle that your heart becomes, the better your endurance and recovery time. Aerobic exercise and a low-fat diet are the keys. For most team sports, we recommend a conditioning program combining running (high impact) and swimming (low impact). Swimming is an especially good workout on low-energy days or when you're trying to rehab from minor injuries. If swimming is not part of the workout you get from your college coach, ask about adding it and then consult a swim coach for a workout to help you achieve your goals.

2 *Strength.* Turning yourself into a bodybuilder is not the answer here. Strength training can be used to tone you up as well as bulk you up. Weight training has become an important part of the conditioning process for almost all athletes, but you need to be very careful about your program. Consult with coaches and trainers before you hit the gym. Here are a few things to consider when working out to increase your strength.

- You want to target the muscle groups most needed for your particular sport. A swimmer will not want the same body type as a linebacker.
- You do not want to hurt yourself due to improper form or overexertion.
- You want to make sure that your muscles get ample opportunity to rest.

3 *Size.* In certain sports, however, bigger is better. And while you can't change your body type or force yourself to grow taller over the summer, a bigger frame will give you more confidence when you start playing against bigger college athletes and also allow you to shrug off more punishment and injury. There are a few key facts, however, that you should always remember.

- Size does not equal strength.
- Size helps *only* if you are strong and mobile.
- Many health food products offer claims of increased bulk. Some work. Some don't. Consult your coach and a nutrition expert before starting any dietary program that includes supplements.
- *Stay away from steroids.* They are against the rules and they can be very harmful—even life-threatening.

4 *Speed/quickness/agility/jumping ability, et cetera.* Added strength will increase your explosiveness and also often increase your ability in the areas of speed, quickness, and so on. Quickness, especially, is one of the intangibles that separates the average athlete from the star. There are a number of things you can do—ask your coach for specifics— that can work to improve your quickness:

- practice drills that require short bursts of movement
    —stop and go
    —lateral movement
    —quick repetitive jumps
    —different types of jumps
    —change of pace
    —change of direction
- remember to concentrate on foot speed *and* hand speed
- anticipate: work on thinking quicker than your opponent

Remember that as you become stronger, more conditioned, and more flexible, your quickness will improve and you will become more durable.

5 *Mental toughness.* The most important and most neglected area pertaining to success in sports, mental toughness does not mean being a tough guy.

Many young athletes don't work hard at their schoolwork because they don't think it will help their athletic performance. They're wrong. The brain needs its exercise as much as the heart, and a keen mind will give you an edge in learning new plays, learning the tendencies of your opponents, interacting with teammates, coaches, and officials, and keeping yourself eligible to compete. The quicker you are able to grasp these concepts, the quicker you will be able to increase your playing time and playing ability. In team sports, the "smart" player will better understand the concepts of team play, and in an individual sport—such as golf, for instance—he/she will be better at creating a shot or understanding and playing the percentages.

Challenging yourself in the classroom will therefore work to improve your mental toughness. But being a good student does not always equate to being mentally tough in athletic competition. If being a good student comes naturally to you, you are going to have to mentally challenge yourself with harder courses, extra assignments, word games, puzzles, vocabulary building, or anything else that exercises your abilities to think fast and think hard.

Mental toughness has nothing to do with talking tough. In fact, many young athletes who talk tough are really just using their mouth to hide their fears and insecurities. Don't try to impress new teammates or your future college teammates by telling them how tough you are and how great a player you are. They'll rightfully take you for a blowhard. Show them how great a player you are by working hard, making big plays, supporting your teammates, and giving credit where credit is due.

Mental toughness can often be a by-product of genetics or your environment. When trying to determine your mental toughness and working toward improving it, here are a few questions you should answer.

- How were you brought up?
- What values did your parents, guardians, and coaches instill in you?
- Are you naturally competitive?
- Do you have to win?
- Do you hate to lose?
- Do you burn to be the best?
- Are you self-motivated?
- Are you a finger-pointer looking to blame others for your shortcomings?
- Are you a clutch performer looking to, and able to, excel when games are on the line?
- Will you be able to perform on the larger stage of college athletics?
- Will you be able to avoid peer pressure?
- Will you be able to stay focused when fatigue and competition start wearing you down?

By answering the above questions, and working to put yourself into competitive situations that continue to test both your actual limits and your imagined limits, you will improve your abilities to perform during stressful situations. Building upon workouts from the preceding four improvement areas, you will improve the strength, skill, and stamina that will boost your confidence to build your mental toughness. Everything fits together. If you feel strong you will believe you're strong, and if you start experiencing success you will believe that that success will continue.

· · · ·

One last important tip: If you are being recruited to play a team sport, ask your coach for a playbook so that you can attempt to learn the plays over the summer.

Your Summer Fitness Program

You should spend three days per week (alternating days and areas) working to improve each specific area. *Example:* On Monday,

Wednesday, and Friday work on size and strength, and on Tuesday, Thursday, and Saturday work on speed, quickness, and agility. Keep in mind that these workouts must be tailored to your specific sport, and also keep in mind when you will be competing over the summer because you don't want to burn yourself out in workouts before a game, match, or meet.

When you start working out by yourself or with a partner, you are going to want to make sure that you are working out as efficiently and effectively as you can. It is important to differentiate between quantity and quality and low-impact versus high-impact exercises. You are also going to want good warm-up and cooldown routines to help minimize stress on (and maximize improvement to) your body. Your coach should be able to provide you with these routines and/or you can consult a recommended physical fitness trainer at a local health club.

You should always try to tailor your summer workouts to your specific needs and goals, but Penn lacrosse coach Ann Sage offers a few general rules of thumb: "You should do some sort of weight training, some type of foundation running, some type of technique work, play in summer leagues, and work on your weaknesses. I like the cross-training. Mix it up. If you spend five hours a day with your sport and only your sport, it doesn't necessarily mean you're going to become a better player. You want balance."

Social Skills
· · · · · · · ·

When you move up to the collegiate level you will be interacting with new sets of friends, teammates, coaches, professors, and advisers. Your world will slowly begin to change itself from a world comprised primarily of teenagers to a world comprised primarily of adults. You will be on your own more. You will have a lot of options to choose from when it comes to your time and your friends. Now you (and not your parents and/or guardians) must govern your life, school, and sport. It's important to be prepared to adjust. Here are some lifestyle changes you should consider over the summer.

Take Responsibility for Managing Your Own Time

During the summer before you start your freshman year, you should try to copy the college experience as much as possible. Ask your parents and/or guardians to cut you some slack for a few days each week during which you manage your time and your diet without any input. After every few days review how much time you wasted, how well you ate, how tired you are, and what you need to do to improve your efficiency and effectiveness. It's going to be difficult for many of you to get your parents to pretend that you're living on your own, but the experiment could pay off—especially while they're still close by to offer advice.

Have Serious Conversations with Your Girlfriend or Boyfriend

If you have a significant girlfriend or boyfriend, discuss how your relationship will be affected by the changes coming at the end of the summer. The first weeks of college can be an exciting and traumatic time. You do not want to get to a new school in a new place and have to deal with unexpectedly getting dumped. Talk things out while you're both together, and make sure that if you choose to continue your relationship that it is strong enough, to withstand being apart. If you are sexually active, always be very careful with your protection so as not to risk any health consequences (sexually transmitted diseases, AIDS) or an unwanted pregnancy which might postpone your college sports plans.

Stay Clean

Avoid all drugs, steroids, and other illegal substances. You do not want to put anything in your body that could hinder your health, your academic performance, your athletic performance, or get you sent to jail. It is important that you do this for yourself and not for anyone else, because when you are on your own you will have to fight the temptations by yourself.

Stay Sober

Watch your alcohol intake. In most states, it's illegal for high schoolers to drink, but that doesn't seem to stop anyone from doing it. If you have a drinking problem you should seek help immediately. It could ruin your life and your health. If you're a social drinker who occasionally likes to have a beer after a game, we recommend that you stop, but if you think you can handle it be very careful to not get drunk or caught. You don't want your judgment impaired by alcohol and you don't want to risk a potential accident. A few hours of fun aren't worth a lifetime of pain and embarrassment.

Have Fun

Warnings aside, it is important to try and have fun during the summer before you go to college. With every passing year, you will be adding responsibilities to your life, and this is a final chance for you to be both a teenager and an adult.

As Olympic swimmer Cristina Teuscher advises, the key to the summer is "just enjoying yourself, not stressing about anything. You shouldn't get all hyped up about school."

Teuscher says you should begin getting ready for your freshman year about two weeks before the start of school "because if you start any earlier you might start stressing out.

"Another good thing," she recommends, "is to wait until you get to school to see what you really need, such as cinder blocks, to put under your bed or a rug—wait until you get to school and you can always buy it when you're there. With getting stuff for school, it's really smart to ask someone who's been to college. I learned through trial and error with my sister. I wanted everything to be new for my room and my sister told me, 'When I got to school I really missed my old sheets at home because they were soft and I had gotten all these new ones.' Her advice was, 'Just take the old stuff and you'll love it.' "

So don't stress. Don't start preparing too early. Don't buy too much and, most important, says Teuscher, "You should just enjoy each day with your friends."

College

Getting Off to a Good Start

A t the beginning of the freshman year you will face many new challenges. You may be away from home for the first time. There will be new living responsibilities, a tougher course load, more free time, and more distractions. You will be making new friends, adhering to a more rigorous practice and training schedule, and learning the ropes from an unfamiliar support group. In this new environment there will be a lot of adapting to do, and it's important for you to get off to a good start.

Preseason Training

Being an athlete at the college level is far more demanding than anything you have encountered in high school. The practices are longer and harder, the competition is tougher, and the season is longer. It is therefore very important for you to build upon the work you've accomplished in the summer with a preseason training regimen.

If you're a fall-sport athlete, your college athletic career is likely to start before you ever see a college classroom. You will therefore have to do as much preparatory work as you can before you arrive at college, so talk to your high school coach and college coach about a fitness program to improve your strength, speed, and quickness. Get advice on what off-season leagues or meets you should compete in to improve your game. But no matter how much training you do over the summer, it will be difficult to prepare yourself for those first college practices. Be prepared to struggle and don't get down on yourself. Understand that returning athletes have a tremendous advantage in terms of preparation and access to your coaches. And remember that all freshmen are in the same boat.

If you're a winter- or spring-sport athlete, preseason training offers you an opportunity to adjust to collegiate life and make significant gains in skill level, conditioning, and strength. Do what your coaches tell you to do. Work harder than your teammates work. Show your new teammates that you are going to be an athlete they are going to have to pay attention to. Use your off-season to meet with coaches as much as the rules will allow to increase your knowledge of your sport and your role in your team's system, and ask your coach for a series of drills and conditioning exercises that will work to improve your consistency and intensity.

Your preseason training regimen needs to be more difficult than your summer training regimen because it must take into account the gains you've made over the summer and also your needs for competing in practice against your new college teammates. The preseason training regimen is divided into three essential areas: (1) diet, (2) strength training, and (3) skill development.

Diet: You Are What You Eat

You're away from home. You eat what you want. You put what you want in your refrigerator. Danger. Repeat. Danger.

You may be young and your athletic body may be able to burn calories at a dizzying rate, but your dietary goal should not be to stuff as many donuts as you can down your throat because you'll burn them off at practice. Your dietary goal should be to eat as well and as nutritiously as you can so that your body will gain strength from your food intake and not be forced to waste energy burning empty calories. Your body will thank you and your skin, still eager to be home to pimples of all shapes and sizes, will also thank you. Now this doesn't mean you can't make occasional late-night runs to the local burger joint (even greasy burgers have protein to go with all that artery-clogging fat) or indulge in an occasional banana split (bananas are high in potassium), but you should start to give some thought to what you are swallowing.

Basic rules of thumb:

- *Avoid the fried stuff.* The fat will clog your arteries.
- *Kick caffeine.* If you find yourself getting tired, try to sleep more and try to sleep and wake at the same time every day. Don't burn and crash.
- *Don't snack on fats* (cakes, ice cream). Empty calories.
- *Drink a lot of water.* You need to stay hydrated and keep your system cleansed.
- *Eat a lot of fruits and vegetables.* Vitamins, natural sugars, and fiber make an athlete stronger.
- *Eat a lot of complex carbohydrates* (grains, pastas, potatoes, etc.). An excellent source of low-fat, slow-burning energy.
- *Keep your sweet tooth in check.* Sugar provides a quick rush of energy *and* a quick loss of energy.
- *Stay away from beer and alcohol.* Not only is it illegal for most of you to be drinking, alcohol is fattening and frequently leads to poor decision making, which can get you arrested, injured, or put on probation.

By sticking to a healthy diet (and combining it with the proper amount of rest), you will find it easier to maintain your conditioning, have a better complexion (for all those TV interviews), be more alert, and feel more energetic.

Strength Training

Your workout should give you specific weight room and aerobic exercises to do on specific days with specific workout partners—and probably with specific supervision. Working out in this structured way will build your strength and stamina and also give you an idea how you compare to your teammates. Do not miss training sessions unless you have an ironclad excuse like a midterm or a serious injury. A runny nose won't cut it.

Skill Development

If the coach does not give you specific skill drills to go with your strength drills, ask. By the time you've arrived on campus your coach should have a good idea what your strengths and weaknesses are and where your abilities need the greatest improvement. Skill drills should work not only to improve basics like quickness and hand-eye coordination but also sport-specific skills like hitting a curveball, mastering a crossover dribble, or serving a volleyball. When you start official practice you want to be able to impress your coaches with something they haven't seen before.

The Key Adjustments Every Freshman Must Consider

• • • • • • • • • • • • • • • • •

In order for you to keep your head above water during that all-important first year of college, you should be aware of certain factors.

The Gap between High School and College

It helps to realize from the start that there is an academic, athletic, and social gap between high school life and college life. Calculus in college, for example, will be more difficult than calculus in high school: the college version will be designed more to prepare you for higher levels of mathematics than the high school version. Your college exams will also be much harder to ace than your high school exams. Some high school teachers want their students to do well so they hand out a lot of As. Most college professors use a "curve" to grade exams so that the majority of the students fall in the middle of the curve and only the very best get As. It is therefore important to devote as much time as possible to strengthening your academic weaknesses.

Athletically, you're also going to meet a much tougher challenge in college. In high school, you may have dominated due to superior strength, game knowledge, or athleticism, but in college you'll be going up against the best of the best of the last four years of high school players. Your usual conditioning regimen and game preparation just won't cut it anymore. Realizing that you need extra work and practice time could be the difference in your making the team, getting playing time, or even starting as a freshman.

Socially, it's important to realize the enormous difference between minimum (high school) and maximum (college) independence. When you're living at home, your parents or guardians usually exert some control over your free time. But in college, you will have more free time—and it will be all your own. In addition, as an athlete, your social behavior will be of interest to your classmates—both those who look up to you and those who wish to bring you down.

Be Careful about Your Academic Scheduling

Select courses that balance and interrelate with each other and with your practice times. You want to take as many courses as possible when you're best prepared to take them: not too early if you like to be up studying late, not after practice when you're too tired to pay attention. If you have trouble writing, you don't want a schedule in which all your courses have essay exams and term papers. If reading bogs you down, you don't want your schedule heavily weighted with literature. And if science gives you nightmares, make sure that you don't take too many science courses during the same semester. Talk to an academic adviser about your abilities, interests, and study habits and work together to devise a schedule that works best for you. It's also recommended that you choose at least two easier courses to lighten the load. One way to do this is to ask older teammates for tips on picking the easier courses. Another way is to look for courses in disciplines in which the course material may overlap so that there are some common themes to your studies.

Example: If you take a history course about America in the 20th century and a political science course about modern American government, a number of the same names, concepts, and facts will be part of both courses. If you take an astronomy course with a physics course, similar mathematical theories may be needed for both. Although you want to get a well-rounded education, you don't always want to get a well-rounded education every semester. Sometimes you want your courses to feed and build off of each other.

Keep in mind that you can almost always experiment with a tough course in summer school, when you'll be under less pressure.

Build Your Academic Maturity

In getting off to a good start, reading and writing fundamentals will go a long way. Talk to an academic adviser to find out what extra help your school might offer in terms of noncredit seminars to improve study habits. Many colleges offer freshman composition classes to improve basic skills or have writing programs in which your papers will be examined and critiqued. It is essential that you practice whatever drills are recommended to you by a writing coach or English professor so that you increase your ability to formulate thoughts and translate them to paper.

In college, you will be bombarded with more reading and writing assignments than you are accustomed to, so the better you are prepared to handle them, the easier your life will be in the classroom, in the library, and in study hall. And the easier your life is in these environments, the more time and intensity you will be able to devote to your athletic performance.

Stay One or Two Assignments Ahead

In handing out their course syllabi, many college professors will inform you of your entire semester's reading and writing requirements. It's to your advantage to stay one up and review as often as possible. Keeping up with the workload will lessen the need for pre-exam cramming, improve your classroom participation (which will score you big points with most professors—especially since many professors don't expect participation from athletes), and give you more confidence at test time.

Seek Tutorial Assistance Early

Do not wait until you flunk an exam or blank out on a paper before you seek some extra help. Acquire a tutor for each class you think might cause you problems. At the very least, make a tutorial contact, so there's someone you can call on in case of a crisis. Many coaches will provide academic tutoring and many universities have tutoring centers, where you can have access to old exams and papers. Also, it's always good to team up in a class with a friend or teammate so you can share notes and ideas and have someone to study with at test time.

Schedule Your Study Time Effectively

Many athletic programs offer mandatory study halls; however, it's important to supplement the existing program with one personalized to your needs. Often it's productive to meet a tutor in study hall, but some students find independent study groups more beneficial than tutors or study halls. Most study programs meet in the afternoons, evenings, or weekends, so you should be able to find time to attend the sessions even when your in-season schedule is especially hectic. To maximize productivity at these sessions, try to arrive rested and with a clear mind. You don't want to schedule a study session a few hours before a big game because you will be focused on the game and not on your studies. Also, remember not to eat a big meal prior to studying. Your body uses up a lot of energy trying to digest food. When you're studying, you want that energy put to more productive use.

Olympic fencer Peter Cox, who spent his undergraduate years at Penn State, wasn't sure what he wanted to study when he started school. He let his studies slide early on, and when he decided that he wanted to go into a business program he found he didn't have the grades. Thanks to fair amount of soul-searching and hard work, Cox eventually got his act together and graduated with a medical degree from Cleveland Chiropractic College—but his early fooling around took some of his academic options away from him.

"Unfortunately, because of my first semester I couldn't go directly into the business program," Cox says, "so screwing up helped to limit my choices."

Learn the Ropes from Upperclassmen

Although there is sometimes jealousy on teams between upper- and lowerclassmen, especially if the lowerclassmen are trying to crack the starting lineup and replace the older players, teammates who are upperclassmen should be an invaluable resource as they have already experienced what you are going through. Check with them for insights, advice, old textbooks, and professor recommendations. Understanding the system and knowing how and when to cut corners is often essential to success. Upperclassmen should be able to tell you what classes and professors to avoid and where you are most likely to find sympathy and success. Upperclassmen should also be able to help you make important alumni contacts. Keep in mind that fraternity and sorority living can also sometimes provide the same service and advice as upperclassmen.

Establish Friendships Early

Although the majority of your friends are likely to come from within your sport, it's important to try to broaden your social base. In order to develop a well-rounded circle of friends, you are probably going to have to work fast: once the season starts you will have little time to socialize, and as your popularity grows (or wanes) it may become more difficult to determine who your real friends are. The sooner you find a few friends you can trust, the sooner you will be able to focus on your double workload as a student athlete.

Maintain Your Momentum

The better you perform in and out of the classroom, the more confident you will become. Getting over your adjustment anxieties and developing confidence are often the real key to getting off to a good start. Momentum will sustain its positive flow once you relax, stay assertive, and seek to maximize your collegiate experience.

Learn to Relax

Dealing with increased pressure and stress is part of growing up. With the stresses of juggling your time, exams, athletic competition, and having a social life, it shouldn't be a surprise that you may occasionally feel worn out and/or overwhelmed. It is therefore important to learn and practice a few relaxation techniques. You can try deep breathing exercises, listening to music, isometric muscle tightening and relaxing, meditation, something offbeat like aromatherapy or hypnosis, or something as simple as taking an afternoon nap. There are many excellent books on stress management available from your library or campus bookstore, and information should also be available from your student health service or guidance counselor. Try several methods until you find the one that works best for you. And don't worry if some of your teammates find your habits odd. If what you're doing helps to keep you happier, more focused, and better prepared to compete, they'll soon be asking you for pointers.

If you find it difficult to relax and frequently find yourself feeling anxious, depressed, and/or unable to sleep, get help. There is no weakness in seeking help, and confidential help will be available for you through your student health service, a guidance counselor, a psychologist, a campus religious leader, or a student support group. Do not let an emotional problem escalate into something serious.

Talk Over Your Problems

Athletes tend not to be especially verbal—especially when it comes to expressing their thoughts and feelings. If you are having problems with your schoolwork, your roommate(s), a college crush, or any other situation which is taking a mental and physical toll on you, find a person to talk to (your roommate, a best friend, a girlfriend/boyfriend, a parent, a coach, or a doctor) and really talk. Don't hold back worrying about what the person might think. There's little that you can tell a doctor or coach that they haven't heard already, and your best friends and parents should want to talk over any topic that might make you feel better. So feel free to rid yourself of any shame and express yourself. It is a good idea, however, to think twice before unburdening yourself to roommates or casual friends. You don't want to put yourself in an uncomfortable living situation, nor do you want your problems to become gossip items in the cafeteria. Make sure that the person you're talking to is someone you can trust.

Trust Your Advisers (but Think for Yourself)

A common problem of this cynical age is an inability to trust. If you seek out a learned professional (say a doctor or adviser) to help you with a problem, it is important to listen to what they say and follow their advice. If you think the advice is bad or they are not really listening to your problem, ask to consult with someone else. You shouldn't follow anyone's advice blindly—especially peers who may mean well but have no idea what they're talking about—but you need to find a few people whom you can trust to provide you with a willing ear and honest, sensible advice.

Choosing the Best Living Arrangements

The best place for you to live should have an environment that is conducive to learning, relaxing, and socializing—each at their own time. Although some universities separate athletes from the general student body and insist they live in special housing and other schools arbitrarily assign you to housing, many schools offer housing options, allowing athletes to choose where they live. Here are some typical options and things to consider about each.

Freshman Dormitories

Freshmen should always live on campus in order to quickly get the hang of collegiate life and have easy access to resources and facilities. In terms of picking a dormitory setup, there are four primary factors to consider: (1) location, (2) size, (3) style, and (4) living arrangements. Here are some questions you should ask yourself to help you make the right choice.

1 *Location.* Is the dormitory centrally located? Is it near the sports complexes, the majority of your classes, the library, and the cafeteria? How easily will you be able to get to your morning classes if you oversleep?

2 *Size.* Dorm rooms come in different shapes and sizes—it's important for you to be comfortable. You will have a locker in your athletic facility, but will you have enough room in your dorm for any athletic gear you like to keep with you? Will you have suitable study space? Are the ceilings high enough and the beds and bathrooms big enough? Don't laugh—many old dormitories were not built to house today's larger, modern-day athlete.

3 *Style.* Depending on the location of the school (city, suburbs, country) and the available land space, living spaces can come in a variety of styles. Will you feel more comfortable living in a true dorm—a few stories high with communal bathrooms—or might you prefer the apartment-style living some schools now offer? Do you prefer old buildings or new? Stairs or elevators?

4 *Living arrangements.* Do you want to live exclusively with athletes or do you want to live with the rest of the student body? Will you feel more relaxed on a same-sex floor or do you want to live on a coed floor? How do you feel about noise and cleanliness?

Check for dormitories that have study and conference rooms, extracurricular programs, live-in professors, student advisers, and teaching assistants. It's important to have as much support as possible during the freshman year.

Generally, freshman student athletes live with their new teammates in either singles (one or two people/one bedroom), doubles (two people/two bedrooms), triples (three people/three bedrooms), or quads (four people/three or four bedrooms). The advantage to this arrangement is support—student athletes have a common experience to share and often suffer similar problems. Unless you have a built-in support group or a desperate need for quiet time, we do not recommend that freshmen live alone in singles because they will limit their social options and miss out on a once-in-a-lifetime style of communal living.

Craig Conlin says that "for the first two years, until you get used to it and really know the ins and outs of college I would definitely recommend dormitory living. I was always very conscious of spending time with 'normal' students as opposed to spending morning, noon, and night with the basketball team. If you spend all your time with athletes, you may start acting a certain way that people really don't look highly upon."

Athletic Housing

Although many schools are trying to get away from the notion of athletic housing, in which athletes live together apart from the general student body, some schools (especially larger schools) still have this option. Similar to a fraternity without the tradition and initiation, athletic housing theoretically allows players the opportunity to bond and coaches the opportunity to police them without outside distractions. If you have an interest in athletic housing or that option is being suggested to you, find out the pros and cons of the housing from coaches and student athletes. If the teams have a lot of money, the athletic dorms may be far superior to the regular dorms in size and appearance, but their location (closer to your practice facilities) might be further from your classes. Although there are some very good reasons for living in an athletic dorm (convenience, study halls, training facilities, etc.), they can be severely limiting.

Living exclusively with athletes can cause sports burnout and force you into an environment with limited horizons. Privacy can also be a problem. To avoid the claustrophobic nature of living exclusively with athletes, we recommend that you seek out group living spaces with private bedrooms in a diverse, coed living community.

Weigh this option carefully.

Fraternities and Sororities (Greek Living)

Freshmen almost never have the option to live in a fraternity or sorority, but the option is worth considering when you get to your sophomore year. Fraternities and sororities can be either on- or off-campus and, to some, they offer a guaranteed social group and a built-in network of connections.

The advantages of Greek living are a tremendous sense of community and support and a guaranteed—virtually unavoidable—social network. But this social network can also be a drawback. Greek living may be fun, and provide you and your team with some instant fan support, but be aware of the dangers of oversocializing and too much partying. And don't allow fraternity peer pressure to force you into a situation in which you're not comfortable. It's great to have "brothers" and "sisters" to stick up for you, but don't let some fraternity initiation procedure or a code of honor make you wake up in a hospital or wind up in jail. Always use your common sense.

One last thing to consider about Greek living is that certain fraternities generally require a large time commitment for meetings, charity work, and social engagements. You may not have any extra time to spare.

College Houses

Some schools also offer college house living programs. College houses are similar to fraternities and sororities in that they foster a strong sense of community and service. The primary differences usually are that college houses are coed, they tend to have a more diverse mix of residents, they have faculty supervision, and you apply to them rather than pledge. If you think you will have any additional time after you're done concentrating on your academics and athletics, a college house may be an option.

Off-Campus Living

Off-campus living is a bad idea for underclassmen, but by the time you're a junior, you'll be acclimated with an established social life, so your priorities will change. What you'll be looking for with regard to your housing will be independence, comfort, and, probably, peace and quiet.

In choosing an off-campus residence, the essential things to look for—in addition to, of course, cost—are safety and convenience. No matter how great the house or apartment, don't move anywhere that will make getting to class or practice difficult, and don't live anywhere you'll feel uncomfortable returning home after a night game or late road trip.

Student athletes with families should either live off-campus or in on-campus residences geared to married couples—usually graduate dorms. Many schools even offer day-care services. Check out your various options with your coach or academic adviser or make an appointment to speak with someone in campus housing or residential living.

Living with a Parent or Guardian

Living at home is not recommended unless it is an emergency. Obviously, if you need to care for a sick relative or your family responsibilities make it essential that you live at home, you have to take that into account. Or if you've been unable to get enough scholarship or financial aid money to cover housing, then that also must be considered. If you already have an established social life and you don't feel you need the activity of life on campus, then that's another reason to stay at home. But an important part of attending college is learning responsibility and independence and learning to deal with new and different kinds of people. If at all possible, we highly recommend living at school.

Picking the Right Courses
· · · · · · · · · · · · · · · · ·

Throughout your academic career, you will need sound advice from four key resources: (1) your parents and personal advisers; (2) upperclassmen and fellow classmates; (3) academic advisers; and (4) coaches. And one of the most important areas in which you can use their expertise is picking the right courses. Says Craig Conlin: "I looked to the older players on the team and they really helped me out. I looked to my academic advisers and they told me the courses I had to take and then I would ask the older players on the team because they knew the system and they knew how to set up a schedule and which professors to take. I think learning the system is as important as gaining knowledge."

Picking the right courses is important because it's the foundation for all your academic work. And as a student athlete you have to pick your classes so that you can best satisfy both your academic and athletic goals. It is therefore important to seek out class-picking help from fellow athletes because they are familiar with the practice schedule, with the travel schedule, and with the reputations of certain classes *and* certain professors.

In picking your classes, you must first think as a student and not as an athlete. Keep in mind these tips.

- In order to graduate, you're going to need to fulfill your school's basic requirements.
- In order to declare and fulfill the requirements of your major, you're going to need specific courses at various levels.
- In order to get a well-rounded education, you're going to want to find courses in areas in which you might be unfamiliar—or even disinterested.

But you must always keep in mind that you have more time commitments, and more athletics-related pressures, than the average student, so you must also factor in a number of other points when mapping out your course load. Here are some questions to ask as you consider your schedule.

- Do your courses meet at times that won't interfere with practice, meals, study time, and sleep?
- Do you have a good balance of challenging courses and (what you hope will be) easier courses?
- Do you have sufficient amounts of study time blocked out in your weekly schedule?
- Will it be better to take any of your courses (especially requirements) in summer school, when the pace is a little slower?

In answering these questions, self-evaluation is very important. *Don't kid yourself* about your own abilities and work habits. If you're a zombie until noon, don't schedule all your classes for the morning.

However, if you have to schedule morning classes because you have afternoon practices, change your habits. Sleep more. Eat better. Party less. You need to be as on your game in the classroom as you are in practice. And if you schedule your day so that you peak at practice, you will certainly suffer in the classroom. Once you start suffering in the classroom, you will probably soon start suffering in practice. Worse, you soon may not be allowed to practice.

So the first thing to consider when picking your classes is you. Talk it over with others and don't tune out what others have to say, but *you know you best*. You don't, however, necessarily know your school and what it has to offer best. Here's where your advisers come in, each with their own areas of expertise—and their own agendas.

A few things to keep in mind regarding these various agendas:

- your parents may want you to take courses that are most oriented toward a promising career;
- your academic advisers, and certainly your coaches, may want you to take courses in which you're more likely to do well;
- your friends may want you to take courses in which you're more likely to help them, by attending class or trading notes.

You have to always keep in mind what your interests and academic goals are because no one is going to do that for you.

Seeking Advice from Your Teammates

A point to remember when seeking advice from your teammates or other upperclassmen is to seek advice from juniors and seniors who have their acts together and are not always one bad grade from probation. Your coach should be able to help you here and hook you up with a teammate who can give you some proper counsel.

Seeking Advice from Your Coach

Your coach should be helpful when it comes to picking classes because your coach, even better than your teammates, should be able to advise you

- on your practice and travel schedule;
- when and if study halls are planned;
- where you can find your best opportunities for tutoring;
- what type of success rate there is for athletes in your chosen areas of study;
- where he or she has contacts on the faculty, administration, and with alumni who might be able to help you academically.

Knowing how your coach feels about classes in conflict with practices will also give you an idea as to the time you can schedule your classes and exams.

Many coaches will watch over your classroom work like a hawk and others will take a more relaxed approach, allowing you to be the adult you want to be. It's important to understand what your coach's approach is so that you don't get trapped down the road—unprepared and ineligible.

Seeking Advice from Your Academic Adviser

Your academic adviser may be the single most important person on campus in terms of getting you through school. Frequently combining equal parts psychology and tough love, your academic adviser should be able to counsel *and* motivate you to do the absolute best that you can in a field of study that will ultimately be the most rewarding intellectually and/or financially.

You should always meet with your academic adviser before choosing your next semester's classes. You should meet with your adviser as often as possible (and needed) during the semester for progress reports, but especially during midterms and finals. If you have trouble or fall behind, this is the person to talk to. *Don't be proud.* The sooner your adviser is aware of a problem, the sooner you can get help. If you feel the need to drop a class or take an incomplete, talk to your adviser.

Your adviser is the person who will make sure you are meeting

- your course requirements;
- your major requirements;
- your graduation requirements.

Your adviser should be able to advise you if a particular course of study may be too much—or too little—for you to handle. If your school has a pass/fail option on certain courses, your adviser should be able to explain how you may best use it to your advantage. Your adviser can explain the benefits of summer school, if that is a realistic option for you, and whether your school will accept summer courses from other institutions in case you want to return home or take a class or two someplace else. But make sure you check this out before you take the class—not all classes are transferable.

Remember, summer school is not only for making up classes. Use your summer sessions to stay ahead.

Talk to your adviser at length before choosing your major and listen, really listen, to what he or she has to say. By the time you pick a major, your adviser should have a good understanding of your interests and abilities and should be able to offer perspective and insight regarding your decision. And if your goal is to continue your education in graduate school, your adviser can help set up a schedule that will best prepare you for a graduate school program, be it medicine, law, business, or any other program.

Since you are depending on this person to help you make so many important decisions, it is essential that you have an excellent relationship with your academic adviser. If you don't click, ask for another adviser. If you still don't feel comfortable, talk to your teammates and coaches about various advisers and find one you can trust. When picking your courses and determining your academic future, trust in your adviser is essential.

Choosing the Right Professors

Every student athlete should try to speak to a professor before a class begins to get an idea how the class is set up. Is it a large lecture or a small seminar? Are there a lot of short quizzes or a few big exams? Are there a lot of papers to write? You want balance here.

Another thing to consider when choosing a professor is to try to avoid professors who have shown an unwillingness to work with student athletes in the past. If you're a football player who has to take a specific math course and one professor who teaches it is a fan and the other despises the idea of collegiate football, you would be a fool to take the course with the second professor. Don't be a fool.

Preparing a Proper Schedule

When thinking about mapping out your courses, think about it as if you were mapping out a schedule for your team. You would want proper rest in between games (meets or matches) and you would not want all your toughest competitions in a row. Long term, you would not want to throw a young, inexperienced team to the wolves—you would want your sports schedule to improve as your team got more maturity and experience. That's the way you should approach your class schedule—as a mixture of challenge and balance spread over four years, one semester at a time.

Don't Take the Easy Way Out

It is important to emphasize here that even though you will get advice about avoiding specific killer courses or hated professors, your goal when picking your courses and planning your curriculum should not be to slide through college working and learning as little as possible. That's cheating yourself and it's cheating the people who have sacrificed to get you there.

That said, it doesn't make sense to put undue (and unnecessary) pressure on yourself if you can avoid it by seeking advice and doing some homework. It is not cheating yourself or the system to balance your course load, to opt for courses that interest you, and to choose professors that will be inclined to help you.

So if you're a spring athlete who is a communications major and you have to take two math and two science courses, courses that will be difficult for you, in order to fulfill a requirement for graduation, don't take all four at the same time—and certainly don't take them in the spring, when your athletic schedule is toughest.

Making an Impression in Practice
· ·

You're on the team and practice has started. Now you want to look good. Whether you're a star recruit or a walk-on, practice is where your coach first gets to see what kind of athlete you are, how hard you work, and how well you listen. Practice is where you get to make an impression . . . and there's a lot you need to know.

The first thing you need to know is that practice is *not* a democracy. Your opinion means little and your coach is not likely to want to hear it.

The second thing is that practice is not fair. A big recruit or star player is going to tend to get the benefit of the doubt over a bench player or walk-on. You can bust your butt and outperform the star on a regular basis, but it doesn't mean that you're a star or even that you're going to get a chance to play. Coaches have set opinions about a lot of things and they tend not to be the most flexible human beings. If the coach wasn't that high on you as a high school player or as a freshman at the end of the bench, it's unlikely that he/she is going to wake up one morning and admit that he/she figured you completely wrong. You may bust your butt for four years and all you may have to show for it is a sore butt. That, however, doesn't mean you shouldn't bust it. You may move up a few spots on the bench; you may prove to be an important practice player who helps the starters (and therefore the team) improve; you may improve your physical fitness, your confidence, and your abilities; you may win the respect of your teammates and coaches, and you may have a lot of fun. You may also be the rare individual who makes him-/herself a collegiate star.

But if you are star, you shouldn't expect a free pass at practice either. Some coaches may ride you harder because you're their meal ticket. Some teammates may compete against you tougher because they want to be the star. In team sports, the opposition coaches are going to be making plans to stop you, so you have to be prepared to make adjustments in practice. And a lot of people are going to be hoping you fail, especially if you show up with a lazy attitude or a big head, which makes your practice time all the more important.

The third thing is that coaches can make you or break you. We've seen frequent examples of good players who seemed to be trying but always looked terrible in practice. Watch them at the end of a game (when they finally get a chance to play) or in a summer league or working out by themselves and you can't figure out how they are playing behind other players thought to be inferior. But then you watch them in practice and they're getting their heads handed to them. This can happen for a number of reasons.

- They might be new, and slower to learn the plays.
- They might be used to a different type of style and be having trouble adjusting.

But,

- They might be playing with an overmatched second unit and be trying to overcompensate, thereby leaving themselves out of position.
- They may be asked to play out of position because their best position might be the same as one of the coach's favorites and the coach doesn't want to move that player.

Key tip: Coaches play who they want to play. You have to make yourself one of the people the coach wants to play.

Craig Conlin played basketball for the excitable Speedy Morris at La Salle and now works as a high school coach. His advice for making a good impression is to always give your all.

"If you make a mistake," Conlin says, "and you're giving it a hundred percent, the coaches will try to help you out and correct it. But if you're making a mistake and you're only giving fifty percent—you're not really trying—then you're not going to be playing much. You're going to be on the bench. And that might cause your relationships with your teammates or coaches to turn sour. But if you're out there and you're aggressive and you're trying your hardest' and you're really trying to improve, you will get support—and I think professors feel that way, too. If you're in the classroom making a real good effort they're going to look after you, they're going to give you some extra work on the side and help you out in any way that they can. But if you don't want to try then they're just not going to give you the time of day."

Conlin's other tip pertains to airing your dirty laundry in public: Don't. "If you have problems with someone else on the team, you should talk it over with a friend on the team, take your problem right to the teammate and try to work things out that way. Maybe talk to a brother or sister at home or a parent. If that still doesn't seem to work out your problems, then take it to a coach." But in private.

The Top 20 Practice Tips

For the star, the benchwarmer, and every level of athlete in between, practice time is essential. It's when you get to know your teammates strengths and weaknesses and your coaches' strengths and weaknesses. If you pay attention to the group dynamic of a practice and how the coaches treat various players and how various players act around each other, you should learn a lot about what you'll need to do. Figure out who the coaches' favorites are and determine what those people are doing that you may not be doing. It's not always going to be that the favorites are merely better than you. They may have a better attitude—that means an attitude that jives with the head coach's attitude. They may be doing little things, like correctly switching defensive assignments, that don't show up in statistics. Little things frequently mean a lot. Especially in practice.

20 Tips

Here are 20 tips to make yourself a better practice player, which should help you become a favorite of any coach. Some of these tips are what coaches, announcers, and reporters like to call intangibles. They all apply to team sports but many of them will also apply to student athletes in individual sports.

1 *Be consistent.* Show up every day and practice hard. No runny noses. No hangnails. No mood swings. You're there. You're pumped.

2 *Concentrate.* Practice can be fun but it's serious business. Especially to your coach. Pay attention and, equally important, look like you're paying attention. Nod every once in a while. Make eye contact with whichever coach is talking. Don't chat while the coach is talking. Don't let your eyes wander. And whatever you do, don't roll your eyes or smirk.

3 *Have a winning attitude.* Don't be selfish. Don't whine. You love practice. You live for practice. You will run through a brick wall for your coach. And, if asked, you will build that wall first. With stones that you dug from the ground. With your bare hands. And carried on your back for miles. In the hot sun. Get it?

4 *Hustle.* The coach would like that wall built faster, okay? Even if you are mentally going through the motions, hustle, hustle, hustle. If your heart's not in it, then master "fake hustle"—that's the art of looking like you're a dynamo even if you're not really accomplishing anything. Coaches love players who hustle. Fans love players who hustle. Hustling is good. Hustling and winning? Now you've got something.

5 *Be tough.* No, practice is not a real game, but pretend it is. There aren't any fans present, but pretend there are. Get dirty. Dive for loose balls. Slide hard. Whatever it takes to show your coach you're a gamer. This is very important for freshmen because your college coach has never seen you play a game against this level of competition. Practice is your first opportunity to show you're tough enough.

6 *Understand teamwork.* Support your teammates in word and deed. Cheer your teammates on. If you have a problem with a teammate or with the coach, see the teammate or the coach privately. Do not make a scene in practice. Do not put yourself above the team.

7 *Understand your role.* Ask the coach to define what he/she expects your role to be—starter, key substitute, bench player, practice player, spark plug, bench cheerleader—and then perform that role to the best of your ability. Don't complain. If you believe you deserve a larger role, talk to your coach and then work hard in practice and prove it to your coach.

8 *Master fundamentals.* By the time you get to college, your coaches don't want to have to spend important practice time teaching you the basics of technique and team play. To improve your form, watch professionals, read a book, or work out on your own time with an alumnus, friend, or teammate who can improve your technique. And also ask your coaches for drills that you can do on your own.

9 *Show advanced skills.* If you take the trouble to learn a new move or skill on your own time—summers are great—your coaches will be impressed. In basketball you may want to improve your off hand (that's the hand you don't normally use to shoot). If you're a football quarterback you may want to work on mastering the screen pass or improve the timing and speed of your handoffs. If you're a gymnast or diver you may work on adding an extra rotation or a twist. Ask your coaches what advanced moves you should work on in your free time.

10 *Have a feel for the game.* Knowing when to make a pass, call a time-out, or cut off a throw from the outfield will force a coach to look upon you more fondly. It's very difficult to teach a feel for the game—it's acquired through practice, learning, osmosis, genetics, and other intangibles—but developing a better understanding of positioning, tempo, and situational play will make you a big hit with coaches. Coaches love to talk about a particular player who understands the game. Once in a while, ask a coach to help you break down a game film and discuss various options, situations, and strategies.

11 *Learn quickly.* If the coach demonstrates and you don't get it, that's bad. If the coach demonstrates and within seconds you've mastered it, that's good. You score points with your coach. And you play more. Coaches hate a lot of things—most things, actually—but one thing they hate more than anything is a team member who keeps making the same mistakes. That athlete won't be playing very much—and if the problem continues, that athlete won't be a team member for very long.

12 *Demonstrate big play ability.* Coaches love players who make plays. It makes coaching so much easier when your players can make things happen. Determine what skills you have that you can exploit and aggressively show them off in practice. Make plays.

13 *Motivate yourself.* If your coach wanted to be your psychologist, he/she would have gone for another graduate degree. You can't depend on your coach to instill a hunger within you. If you're not motivated to play—and play hard—maybe you shouldn't play. If you really want to play but don't feel the hunger you think you need to excel, talk to your coach, your adviser and/or your parents or guardians about seeing a counselor, a psychologist, or a sports psychologist.

14 *Arrive early/stay late.* Nothing will endear you to a coach more than being the first player at practice and the last one to leave. If you use this time to work on your weaknesses, you may even see your coach smile. If, however, the coach finds out that you're spending so much time at practice because you're skipping classes, that smile will quickly disappear. And so will you.

15 *Do more than expected.* The same way you would ask a professor for an extra credit assignment to help bring up your grade, you can ask your coach for an extra drill or if he/she needs any help at a local dinner or an alumni function. You don't want to come across as a brownnoser here (or a coach's pet), and nothing is going to help you with the coach if you're just not good enough to play, but showing a strong commitment to the team can have benefits beyond a few extra minutes of playing time should you ever need your coach's help landing a summer job or getting into a course or with an academic problem.

16 *Exude confidence.* If you look like a loser you play like a loser, and if you play like a loser you look like a loser. Body language is important. Don't slouch. Don't sulk. Don't shy away from physical contact. If a teammate tries to get under your skin, give it right back. Even if the coach repeatedly gives indications to you that he/she doesn't think you're good enough, you have to think you are—and you have to practice like you are. And eventually you may win the coach over, too.

17 *Fight through injuries.* No one is going to expect you to be sprinting 40-yard timed dashes with a broken leg, but coaches hate crybabies. They hate players who miss team practice or individual workouts due to assorted nicks, scrapes, twists, pulls, aches, and colds. Coaches are all Abraham Lincoln: When they went to school they walked 10 miles each way, uphill, through the snow, with 20 pounds of books on their back. To your coaches, you're just a wimp— a gutless, pampered wimp. At least until you prove otherwise. So if you have a headache, get two aspirin from the trainer and get your butt to practice.

18 *Demonstrate leadership.* Not everyone on a team can be the captain, but everyone can be a leader. Leading is not just being the loudest player in the pregame meeting or being the first to demonstrate a drill. Leading is doing things correctly, it's supporting a teammate who's down, it's being responsible for your actions at and away from practice. Coaches love players who are mature and responsible, whom they don't have to worry about and don't have to baby-sit. Coaches notice leadership. And so do teammates.

19 *Improve your physique and stamina.* It's relatively easy for a coach to notice stamina: You're out there looking fresh as a daisy while your teammates are dropping like flies. It's not so easy to notice an improved physique because body changes are like changes in your age: When you see someone every day, subtle changes don't register. But if you go years without seeing someone, let's say your Aunt Sadie, then one day you see Aunt Sadie and say (to yourself, we hope), "Gosh, Aunt Sadie got old." If you lift and exercise during the season your progress will not register immediately. But one day in practice one coach will turn to another and say, "Look at Johnnie's arms, he must be lifting."

Improved physiques are, of course, noticeable if you build up over the summer. It's a great feeling showing up for your first practice of the season knowing that all your coaches and teammates will notice how fit and strong you look. But remember: *No quick fixes! No banned substances!* Your body has to last you your entire life. Do not abuse it while it's still young and growing.

20 *Be personable with guests.* Frequently, alumni, boosters, administrators, local high school coaches, and recruits drop by practice. Don't act like a jerk. These are people who support your program (some of them might be able to give you a job when you graduate) and you gain nothing by having them think ill of you. If a visitor is someone you don't know, you're under no obligation to talk to them unless you're introduced, but otherwise you should always say "hello" if the opportunity arises. The little things, again, pay off.

If a recruit is at practice, talk to him/her during breaks. If the coach has not yet picked anyone to show him/her around, then volunteer. If a coach can trust you with a recruit, then you truly are an important member of a team whether or not you ever play a minute, run in a race, or wrestle in a meet.

By paying attention to the 20 tips outlined in this chapter, you will make yourself an invaluable practice player and assure yourself every reasonable chance of scoring points with your coaches. Dave Johnson, however, stresses that when it comes to making an impression, you must understand the reality of human nature.

"The coach will naturally tend to notice a natural athlete," Johnson says. "Athletes just stand out from their peers through their ability. But beyond that, a coach wants to see an athlete who is coachable and that's someone who is willing to try."

In order to make it, Johnson says, "you've got to be willing to do what it takes to be successful and successful doesn't necessarily mean being a conference champion or the starting quarterback. Success is something you have to start measuring in personal terms. It's a matter of improvement. If you're improving, you're successful. Then the question becomes are you improving at a rate you should be improving, which is to say you're meeting expectations. Are you improving at a rate that's below what you should be achieving, which would mean that you're not living up to expectations. That's always very discouraging to a coach. It's actually rare to find too many people achieving beyond what is expected of them, but those are the people that coaches love."

8 Educational Skills

your athletic ability may help you get into *a* college, but it's your academic ability that will help you get into *any* college. And once you're in college, it's your academic ability that will keep you there and help you get as much out of the experience as possible. It is therefore essential to do whatever you can to improve and enhance your educational skills, which include improving your ability to study and learning to manage your time effectively so you don't ever have to concern yourself with losing your athletic eligibility.

Skills to Work On

You want to prepare for your academic work in the same way, and with the same intensity, that you prepare for a game—by playing to your strengths and improving your weaknesses. Here are the areas you need to consider.

● *Work habits.* Learn *when* you are most productive (morning, afternoon, evening, late night) and *where* you are most productive (dorm room, library, empty classroom, outside). Also determine how much time you realistically need to study and set aside the needed time. Avoid distractions such as long phone conversations and watching television, and at all costs avoid procrastination—don't put off for later what you can do now.

● *Ability to concentrate.* Learn how long you can study in a given session before you lose your focus. Schedule breaks. Ask yourself if you study better by yourself or with a classmate? With music or without? With food or when you're hungry?

● *Vocabulary.* The more command you have of the language, the better you will be able to use it for your own needs. In the classroom, words are your tools, and it is important to be able to use as many tools as possible—both in getting your points across and in understanding what is said to you. Many vocabulary books are available, but a good first step is to go through the glossaries of any texts required for your classes and make yourself familiar with the words, names, and phrases that might be relevant to that course. From there you can build your vocabulary in other directions with a dictionary, a book of quotations, an encyclopedia, or even some type of word game or crossword puzzle book.

● *Reading speed.* With all of the reading you are going to have to do in college it should be obvious that the faster you can get through the material the more time you will have to study it and improve your grasp of its facts and concepts. One way to improve your reading speed is to read a lot and make yourself more familiar with the way phrases go together and sentences are structured. Your reading speed will also improve as your vocabulary improves and as you make yourself more familiar with the names and concepts in the course material. But there are also courses you can take, books you can read, and audiotapes you can listen to that will give you pointers on how you can increase your reading speed *and* your comprehension. Check out the Internet or your campus bookstore for ideas or talk to a reference librarian.

● *Writing skills.* Just as you're going to have to do a lot of reading, you are also going to have to a do a lot of writing—assignments, research papers, and exams, for example. If you can write quickly and coherently, you will be able to produce your papers faster, better, and with less anxiety, and leave yourself more time for other work (and play). It is very good idea, therefore, to take a course in expository writing during your freshman year. A course like this will help you with sentence structure, focusing your thoughts, getting your ideas down on paper, and research techniques. It could be invaluable. It is also helpful to talk to your professors about your writing and ask them for ways to improve. They will be more likely to cut you some slack if they see you are interested and they may also provide you with some drills or reference materials that will help.

● *Communication.* If you've improved your vocabulary and your ability to read and write, that should go a long way to improving your communications skills. But one other key element to communication is confidence. You may be loud and opinionated with your friends but clam up in the presence of a professor, either because you do not have confidence in your ability to understand the information being taught you or you do not have confidence to express yourself in the language of the classroom—as opposed to the language of the street. Practice—either in front of the mirror, with a tape recorder, or both. Public speaking may not be in your future, but the need to speak in public will be. If you have this fear and you master it, you will find that this new confidence will spill over into other areas as well.

With these skill sets in place, the next key area to focus on is time.

Managing Your Time
on Campus and on the Road

As we've stated before, managing your time is a key to your success. You're going to have more time and more temptation than you've ever had before, so it's important to be organized so that you don't let any bad habits overwhelm you—because you're also going to have more work to do.

Going away to college is both a big responsibility and a big tease. You're placed in an environment with countless people your own age and given all kinds of freedom, but you're also given just enough work to force you to impose some structure on that freedom. There is plenty of time for fun in college, but if the fun takes over, your work (and your athletic career) will suffer. Your goal is to achieve a balance and harmony between your work, your practice, and your play.

"You have to manage your time," says Georgia basketball great Saudia Roundtree. "Basketball takes up a lot of time but you have mandatory study halls, which I think a lot of the coaches have their players go to. But as far as studying, you have to do that on your own. You have to make time. That goes back to discipline. You have no social life whatsoever when you play sports because you just don't have time."

Basketball star Tom McMillen won a Rhodes scholarship after graduating from Maryland, but even he says "the only way I got caught up was by studying on weekends, and a lot of college kids don't want to do that—but that's what you're going to have to do if you're going to succeed."

A typical high school day is wake up, go to school until around 3 or 4 P.M., go to practice, go home, eat dinner, study, watch TV, talk on the phone, go to sleep, have fun on the weekends. Your days are almost completely structured. And road trips rarely go overnight.

College is completely different. Practice could be in the middle of the day or in the morning. On some days you might have *hours* of spare time *between* classes. You will probably have two to three times the schoolwork. You will probably have roommates whose schedules differ from yours and will want to have fun when it's convenient for *them*. No one will be checking on you to make sure you eat well or get enough sleep. And road trips frequently go overnight. In some of the major athletic programs, you can be away from school for days at a time.

In addition, for probably the first time, you are going to have to handle personal administrative tasks like registering for classes, buying your books, picking a place to live, choosing times to eat your meals, and so on. For some of you, this may be the first time you have your own checking account and must balance your own checkbook. All of these things take time and must be figured into your time management schedule.

The key word here is *schedule.*

"As a student athlete, you've got to keep in mind what your commitments are," says former lacrosse all-American **Scott Gabrielsen,** "especially in the afternoon. To go directly from a late afternoon class straight to practice is probably not the best idea because you're going to be rushing the whole time and you're not going to be able to focus on your sport. And while you're in class you're going to be too preoccupied thinking about practice and how you're going to get there and you're going to take away from your studies. You ought to give yourself an hour or two between that last class and your practice and try not to schedule any class after practice where you'd have to leave early. You have to be one hundred percent focused on each one of the things that you're doing, whether it's sitting in a class or being on the practice field."

How to Schedule Your Time

First, buy yourself a daily planner. If you can't afford one, ask your coach or someone in your athletic department if there are any extras lying around because planners are frequently given out as gifts. If not, ask your student bookstore if they have any free samples in new student orientation packets. It doesn't have to be fancy. It just has to have a page or two per day with the hours blocked out. You can even make one on a computer or a few pieces of graph paper.

Next, write down the times you have classes, informal or formal practice sessions, workout sessions, and study halls. These are blocks of time that are committed so you don't have to worry about filling them. See when you have free time left. See where on campus you will be when you have free time. If you are on a small campus where almost everything is close together, getting from place to place is easy. But if you are at a big university with lots of land, academic buildings, sports arenas, and libraries can be quite far apart—and getting from practice to the library may be a line in your planner but may actually take 15 or more minutes.

So based on your schedule and location, when is it most convenient (and efficient) to work out? When is it most convenient to meet with advisers? When is it most convenient to work in the library? And when is it most convenient to work in your room? You don't want to waste half of your study time walking back and forth to your dorm when you're two minutes away from the library or a perfectly adequate empty classroom.

Now, write yourself a weekly schedule. Keep in mind, except for the classes and practices and mandatory meetings, this schedule is not etched in stone. It is simply a blueprint for your week so that you leave as few things as possible to chance.

In addition to a weekly schedule, you should also write yourself a "Things to Do" list each day. Jot these items down as they occur to you. Don't leave errands (such as: 1. do laundry tonight; 2. call bank to see why checks haven't arrived yet; 3. buy toothpaste) to chance or to your memory or you'll return home from a tough day, forget, and wind up with no clean clothes, no way to pay your bills, and no pearly whites. Besides, you want to tap that brainpower for your schoolwork. Also, by spending a few moments each morning thinking about your day and your route through campus, you'll pack your knapsack, briefcase, or bag with everything you need and not realize that your Econ book is sitting on your desk in your dorm room as you're casually strolling to the class.

In the "In Season" section of this chapter, which follows shortly, you will find a sample schedule. Adapt it to your own needs and time commitments.

And then stick to it.

• • • •

When mapping out your time, there is one other thing you should consider: whether you are (1) preseason, (2) in season, or (3) postseason.

"When I was in season," says former La Salle basketballer Craig Conlin, "that's when I did the best in school because I always felt that I had so little time for anything that I had to set my mind to do things. I'd get up in the morning, hit class, practice in the afternoon, and then usually had a couple hours at night to get homework and projects and papers done. Then the next day, the whole process begins again. Whereas when you're out of season, you don't have practice in the afternoon and you feel like you have all the time in the world and nothing ever seems to get done. So when I had constraints on my time I really seemed to do better in school because I knew that I only had a certain amount of time to do things. It's keeping your mind focused, staying organized, and that comes from getting help from older players and your academic adviser and not procrastinating. Get things done and get them out of the way."

Preseason

With different sports playing during different seasons, there are three distinctive and very different preseasons to consider.

1   If yours is a fall sport, you should use your summer to get ahead. Here are some suggestions.

- Build up your strength and stamina so that the first days of practice (in the summer heat) don't wipe you out.
- Try to get reading lists for your fall classes and do some of the reading before you get to school.
- Get as many school-related errands (purchasing books, registering for classes, sorting out housing arrangements, meeting with advisers, etc.) completed as soon as possible so that you don't waste too much precious time once you arrive on campus.
- If you are a freshman (or transfer), walk around campus and learn the best routes to and from your classes and the approximate times it takes to walk, bike, or ride places. Get acclimated.

2   If yours is a winter (or spring) sport, the fall should be a time when you

- get accustomed to the time commitment of preseason workouts and begin anticipating the additional burden of in-season workouts;
- take a heavier course load in case you need to drop a course when you are in season;

- learn your in-season practice and game schedules and use that knowledge when you pick your spring class schedule.

3 Spring sports athletes should draw upon the tasks of both the fall and the winter athletes, but add one significant helper:
- Don't waste your Christmas vacation. Sure you're entitled to have fun, but the great benefit to playing a spring sport is you have the whole first semester plus Christmas to set up a strong academic foundation.

In Season

Yes, getting everything that you need to get done is tough during your season, but if you get ahead in the preseason and give yourself a bit of a cushion, you should be able to scrape together enough time to get by.

The most important thing you can do during the season is to follow the schedule you've written in your daily planner. A sample schedule might go something like this (you have to incorporate your own class times and practice times).

1 7 A.M.: Wake up, shower, dress.

2 7:30–8:30 A.M.: Review yesterday's notes, prepare for that day's classes.

3 8:30–9 A.M.: Breakfast. You can move breakfast time up before your review session if you need some food before thought.

4 9–11 A.M.: Morning classes. Try to schedule classes when you're best able to able concentrate. Also, try not to schedule too many classes back to back—you'll start fading out after a while.

5 11 A.M.–noon: Meet with professors, advisers, or coaches. Run errands.

6 Noon–1 P.M.: Leisurely lunch with friends. Get gossiping and sniping out of the way now. If possible, incorporate some talk about classes or future classes into this time.

7 1–2:30 P.M.: Afternoon class. On days you don't have this much classroom time blocked out, use this time to study in the library.

8 2:30–3:30 P.M.: Relax. Go back to your room and lie down. Put on some soft music, watch some TV, or read a magazine. Closing your eyes isn't a bad idea, but make sure you set your alarm so you don't miss practice. If you need to see your trainer or get a massage, now is the time.

9 3:30–4 P.M.: Prepare for practice. Get dressed, taped, whatever. Go over probable plays or drills. Work on your form—whatever your sport (and practice for your sport) dictates. If your coach is someone who measures your dedication by how early you arrive at practice and how late you stay, you'll have to take a little less relaxation time here so that you ensure a little more playing time later.

10 4–6:30 P.M.: Practice. This is your coaches' time. Pay attention.

11 6:30–7:15 P.M.: Unwind, shower, speak to your coaches about any potential problems, or scheduling conflicts, or practice plays or movements that are troubling you. Now is a chance to get some individual instruction.

12 7:15–8 P.M.: Dinner. Replenish your fluids and eat a good meal, but not too much. You don't want to fall asleep when you . . .

13 8:00–10:30 P.M.: . . . Study. In your room, in the library, or at a friend's—wherever you are least likely to be disturbed and most likely to be productive. Two to three nights a week during this time you should work with your coach and/or adviser to schedule a study hall.

14 10:30–Midnight: This is your time. A nice idea would be to call your parents or guardians, catch up with old friends, or make plans with new friends.

15 Midnight–7 A.M.: Sleep.

Although you're not going to need seven hours of sleep every night and are rarely going to get seven hours of sleep if you do, you will probably need more sleep than you leave time for, so you might as well schedule a reasonable bedtime and then push it back if you find yourself with energy to burn. If you tell your coach that you're just not feeling tired at the end of your day, we're sure your coach will take care of that problem for you.

On the weekends, you have extra free time where your classroom blocks normally are and a lenient coach might even give you a day off from practice. You should use this time to rest, study, and have fun. You should, however, try to stay close to a consistent bedtime and wake-up time. Partying should always be in moderation, especially for the student athlete and especially in season. Losing control on the weekends may be a tempting way to alleviate in-season stress, but it can cost you big-time with a physical illness, a suspension, or—worse—an arrest.

By creating an in-season schedule like the one above (adding in your own personal modifications) and then sticking to it, you will find yourself rested, able to make your classes, and with time for meals, study, and practice. You'll find time to have fun. Everybody does.

Postseason

If your postseason occurs when you are still at school (that is, if you're a fall or winter athlete), then you should keep to your in-season schedule as much as possible. Merely allot your scheduled practice time to workout time and additional study time. Just as you used your preseason to get ahead in your classwork, you should use your postseason to

- catch up on any classes in which you may have fallen behind;
- finish any incompletes as quickly as possible;
- talk to your coaches about what you need to do to improve in the off-season.

If you are a spring athlete whose postseason comes in the summer, you can

- finish any incompletes as quickly as possible;
- talk to your advisers about whether you should attend summer school;

- talk to your coaches about what you need to do to improve in the off-season;
- talk to your coaches about summer leagues, camps, clinics, or jobs.

The keys to your summer and the summer of every student athlete are to

1 stay in shape;
2 improve your skills and physical conditioning;
3 improve your mind;
4 relax;
5 have fun.

On the Road

When you're on the road for away games, you cannot let travel and hotel time go to waste. Travel time—whether it's by bus, train, or plane—is a good time to catch up on reading, sleeping, or mentally preparing for the game, race, or meet ahead. When you reach your destination, find out if and when you're going to have a practice session, a film session, a team meeting, or a scheduled meal and make yourself a short schedule to substitute for your schedule at home. Try to stick as closely as possible to your normal schedule so that you get your schoolwork done. If you're traveling across time zones, take that into account when you sleep so you don't throw your body clock out of whack. To maximize your athletic performance on the road, you want your routine before a road game to attempt to duplicate your routine before a home game.

Here are a few important school things to remember before you hit the road.

1 Make sure you pack the right books, notes, pads, pens, and a calculator, if needed.

2 Talk to any professors whose classes you're going to miss and find out the writing and reading assignments. If an assignment is due when you're gone, ask the professor when you need to get it in. If an

exam is scheduled for a day you're gone, find out when you're going to have to take it. It could be as soon as you get back, so be prepared to use your road trip to study.

3 Ask classmates to take notes for you for the classes you are going to miss.

Maintaining Your Athletic Eligibility

When it comes to your athletic eligibility, there are NCAA standards, league standards, and school standards, and one of the first things you should do is find out from your coach or academic adviser what standards you will be asked to adhere to. If you are a scholarship athlete, also find out how your eligibility status will affect your scholarship. Your goal in college is to learn, mature, and prepare yourself for the future, but if you're an athlete you probably also want to play. By maintaining your eligibility you get the opportunity to do both.

At some schools, you as a student athlete will basically have to dare a professor to flunk you—so important are athletics to the school. But at most schools you should not expect any slack. You are going to have to carry your own load. Still, if you treat your professors and teaching assistants with the proper respect and put in the effort in the classroom, most will give you a fighting chance to succeed.

The key to maintaining your eligibility is to stay up on your work. Don't fall behind. If you have daily reading assignments, do the reading daily. Don't leave it all for the weekend because then you'll want to have fun. If you know that a paper is coming up in four to six weeks, don't leave all your reading and researching until the day before—that will be a mistake you will pay for.

If you're taking a course that only has a midterm and a final, you have more opportunity to get your work done in an orderly fashion, but you also have less room for error. When you only have two exams, you have to make those two grades count. Use the weeks before and between exams to get to know your professor and/or TA (teaching assistant), meeting them every two weeks or so to discuss the class, your participation, and the relevant information for the exams. If you are forced to miss a class, talk to the professor about what you missed. Also, show the professor your notes in order to clear up any uncertainties. Doing these things will not only help your chances for a good grade, they will also show the professor that you are committed to doing well—which will in turn improve your chances for a good grade.

Another key to a good grade is good note taking. You should therefore always have up-to-date notes and refer to them between exams so that they stay fresh in your mind. If you're forced to miss a lecture due to an away game, make sure you get photocopies of the notes. If you think your notes are lacking, ask another student if you can photocopy their notes or ask the professor if you can tape the class. By taping a class, you can free your mind up in class to listen and write down what's interesting as opposed to feeling compelled to take down everything the professor says. Taping a class also allows your mind to wander during the class and gives you a chance to relisten to the class when you might be more awake or more focused. It also allows the professor's words to make a second—and hopefully more lasting—impression on you.

In many sports, learning a playbook is essential. You should approach your textbooks as you might your playbook. You would never consider putting your playbook up on a shelf and referring to it the night before a big game, but that's what many of you will do with your notebooks, bringing them out the night before a big exam.

To avoid these potential pitfalls, schedule daily study time and stick to a daily study regimen. You wouldn't think of missing a scheduled varsity practice, so don't miss your daily study session.

College is already more work than you're accustomed to so you have to be more prepared than ever. Once you have set your study times, you want to make sure that you get everything possible out of the sessions. Your time is valuable, so you don't want to waste these sessions due to laziness, inefficiency, or anxiety over the amount of work that lies before you. You can do it. People a lot dumber and lazier than you have graduated college. Calm your fears by breaking down your classwork as if it were a game plan.

- Categorize the main subjects as if these subjects were your opponent, then plan how to beat your opponent.
- Review your notes on a regular basis just as you would your playbook to become familiar with your plays.
- Drill the important subjects into your head, as if these drills were to improve your foul shooting, your golf swing, or a gymnastics routine.
- Participate in study groups as if they were practices. These are not social clubs or opportunities for you to kill time and gossip. Imagine that these study groups are run by your coach in order to cut out the nonsense.
- Try to find mock exams or old exams to practice on. These are your exhibition games.

Other suggestions for maintaining your athletic eligibility:

- Look for alternative resources explaining your class material. Sometimes you may be better able to understand a different perspective.

- Participate as much as possible in class. If it's a lecture class in which participation is not required or recommended, then ask questions of the professor afterward. You want the professor to see you as a student first and as an athlete second. Then, if you need help later on in the semester, the professor is more likely to give you a fair shake.

- Clear up incomplete assignments as quickly as possible to keep your semester grades current.

- Clear up incomplete classes as quickly as possible after the semester ends. Since you will be required to fulfill a specific number of credits each term, you want to receive credit for every class you take in the proper marking period.

● If you feel as if you are being unfairly graded, talk to the professor. He or she might be able to give you an explanation that will help you adjust your work (or your expectations), or you might be asked to do some extra work to bring your overall work up to a satisfactory level. If you get no satisfaction from your professor, see your coach or academic adviser. Do not let a perceived injustice slide until it is too late to do something about it.

● Request extra credit assignments when possible. Remember, it's your average that counts. If you're doing well in a class and an extra assignment can boost your grade, that may soften the blow of a course that you're finding difficult.

● Discuss an exam strategy with your academic adviser. If necessary, ask a professor if you can retake an exam. Occasionally, you may have to ask a professor if you can postpone an exam that you are completely unprepared for. Some professors will agree to this, others will throw you out of their office. That's why it is important for you, your adviser, and your coach to know your professors.

● If your school offers a pass/fail option in some courses, use this option to your advantage. Consult your adviser.

If you stay on top of your game in the classroom the way you do in your sport, you should have no problem staying eligible throughout your college career. All you have to do is:

1 Plan your class schedule wisely.
2 Pay attention to your professors, coaches, and advisers.
3 Study.
4 Treat exams and papers as if they're your archrival. Play to win.

Declaring Your Major
· · · · · · · · · · · ·

At some point in your collegiate career, depending upon the rules of your particular school or conference, you are going to have to declare a major. Your major is a concentrated course of study in a particular area that will eventually lead to your degree and the expertise you hope will land you a job. Majors can be science-related (biology, chemistry, physics, etc.), social science–related (political science, African-American studies, sociology, etc.) or humanities-related (English, history, music, etc.). A major can be in a field of business study that leads to a corporate job, in a field of math or science that leads to a research job, or in a field of humanities that leads to a teaching job. Or you can be a total maverick and take an undergraduate degree in music and try to land a job on Wall Street or go to medical school (as long as you've taken the required science courses).

Your major can lead you to a career in practically anything as long as you do well enough to leave your graduate school options open, should you choose to continue for an advanced degree.

Craig Conlin says, "Rarely do people know what they want to do with the rest of their lives when they're coming out of high school. I would recommend going with the liberal arts group the first one or two years and taking a good base of courses and then after that hopefully you'll have a little more feel for what you want to do. For a major you should consider the course that you seemed to enjoy the most and something that you always dreamed about. Something you'd be good at. Something you would enjoy every day."

Herschel Walker: "I always wanted to be a policeman. I always wanted to be in criminal justice. But at Georgia I had an opportunity to delve a little bit into the criminal justice field and that opened my eyes toward law. Then I said maybe I want to go toward law school. So I knew I had to learn a little bit more.

"You have to learn and memorize and go to the library a great deal. I always tell people that going to the library opens your eyes because you read things you wouldn't ordinarily read sitting in a dorm room."

The important things to remember when picking a major are:

● *Don't rush.* Generally, a major must be declared by the middle of your sophomore year. However, if you are making satisfactory progress toward your degree and you're taking enough high-level courses, you may be able to buy yourself a little more time if you are unsure of yourself. There is no real need to declare a major as a freshman unless you want to get it out of the way, but your mind may change as you expose yourself to more areas of study.

You may think you have an idea of what you want to study when you get to college, but the reality of studying the topic on the collegiate level may be different than you have imagined. Topics that you are interested in when you're 17 often change by the time you're 19 or 20 and you've been exposed to more knowledge and have taken a serious look at the job market and/or graduate schools. Also, when you're 17 you may still be clinging to the unrealistic idea that you're going to make millions as a professional athlete. By the time you're a sophomore, that idea may have been beaten out of you and you may have begun wondering if you're going to have to move back home after college.

● *Don't be influenced by peer pressure.* The worst reason to pick a particular major is because your roommate did, your best friend did, some girl or boy you're hot for did, or the team captain did. You shouldn't pick a major because your coach recommended it or because your academic adviser recommended it or because your parents or guardians recommended it, although you should listen to their reasoning and factor it into your decision.

● *Pick a major you're interested in.* Sounds obvious, right? You would be amazed how many student athletes don't do it, either because they rush into their decision, don't think about their decision, or because they're trying to please or impress someone else. Completing the requirements for your major will dominate your classroom and study time during your junior and senior years and you want that time to be exciting and interesting. You don't want your major classes to be drudge work, so you want to major in a subject that you will want to know about. Other factors, however, occasionally must be considered. Folklore may fascinate you, but there aren't many jobs in folklore—especially lucrative jobs. You may feel pressure from many sides about picking a major that could lead to a high-paying career or a place in the family business. You might have dreams of a mansion and Mercedes, and so you'll also want to factor your ambition into your decision—not to mention your tolerance. Mom may want you to be a doctor but the sight of blood may sicken you. What do you do? Talk over your decision with the people you trust and research the job markets, starting salaries, and grad school options in the library or with your academic adviser. Then choose the major that you believe best meshes your area of interest with prospects for a secure future.

If you are especially ambitious in the classroom and believe you can handle a heavy workload, you may wish to consider the dual major option. Being a dual major allows you to major in both a career-related field and a field of interest (if those two should be different), it allows you to concentrate on disciplines that may greatly enhance your ability to get into a top grad school, and it also may allow you to keep your future options open by concentrating in two distinctly different fields and seeing where your interests take you.

Another possibility, if you are concerned that an area of great interest will not necessarily lead to great job prospects, is to minor in a subject you love and major in a subject that's more practical. This allows you still to get a thorough education in a desirable topic and still sets you up with the potential for a stable career.

"It's something players don't like to do," says former NBA veteran/congressman Tom McMillen, "but if you're interested in medicine, you should go talk to the people who are involved in medicine. If you have an academic interest, you should talk to people who are involved in your academic interest."

● *Pick a major in a field of study you're good at.* If math has been giving you trouble since first grade arithmetic, it's probably not a wise idea to be a math major. If you find writing a paper the equivalent of having a tooth pulled, it's probably best to major in something other than English. When choosing a major, in addition to picking a subject you like, make sure you pick a subject you can do.

Yes, college offers an opportunity to experiment, but just as you wouldn't practice a new athletic skill in the final seconds of a close game you don't want to use your major as a chance to get acquainted with an area of study in which you have always struggled. With a full course load and a full practice schedule, you're not going to have time to learn the skills needed to pass your major and also take the classes. Experiment in summer school or when you believe you have a light schedule. And never experiment with more than one class in any semester.

● *Check the major's requirements.* This will take just a few minutes of your time but it is very important. Some majors require courses that are only given at certain times, which may conflict with your athletic schedule. Some majors require more courses than others and you may not be able to handle an increased workload. Lastly, some majors, and the students and professors who work within them, are not considered athlete-friendly. Ask the upperclassmen how certain classes and professors stack up before embarking on a two-year course of action you will soon regret.

Other things to consider when picking your major:

● *How you will fit in with the other majors and in the graduate talent pool.* Do other athletes major in the field you have chosen? Is it a geek/brainiac major? Do you feel as if you will be able to do well enough in the major that you will stand out if you apply to graduate school?

● *Whether there is money available for graduate school, if that is an option.* While there is frequently money available for humanities majors who wish to continue on for a master's or a doctorate, there isn't often money (except loans) available for med school, law school, and business school. If you are choosing via your major to embark on one of these paths, are your parents/guardians prepared to pay or are you aware of the financial hardship you will endure with the possibility of the financial payoff at the end?

● *The individualized major.* One last option to consider is the individualized major in which you design a course of study from a variety of different course areas. The individualized major allows you to target your areas of interest, but putting together the major and then getting it approved by your school requires a fair amount of work and nervous tension waiting for the answer. This option is definitely not for everyone.

The important idea to remember throughout your college career is to not turn your back on topics that interest you. Find a way to fit them into your academic schedule. And try to take as broad a curriculum as possible, approaching each course with an open mind. You never know which class, text, or professor will provoke your interest and propel your thoughts in exciting new directions.

People Skills

With your athletic skills working in conjunction with your educational skills, you are ready to make your mark in your sport and in the classroom. The last set of skills you need to round out your personal package are people skills—the ability to get along with your coaches, teammates, and teachers and the ability to deal with the media, the alumni, and both the good and bad which may befall you.

In the long run, gaining the respect, trust, and friendship of your teammates, coaches, and alumni may garner you more positives than any grade you receive or any point you score. People skills last you your whole life.

Dealing with Your Coaches

To the average fan, a collegiate coach is someone to boo when the home team doesn't play well. But collegiate coaches have many responsibilities besides cursing at officials. These responsibilities include:

156

- recruiting
- scheduling
- working with the university administration
- conducting practices
- interacting with alumni
- fund-raising
- scouting
- running camps
- dealing with the press
- strategizing
- promoting their team
- dealing with their players
- winning

It's important for you, the student athlete, to fully understand these roles, how they're carried out, and how you may fit into them. By the way, if that last point—winning—isn't achieved, the others won't matter as much.

At the collegiate level, people like to believe that coaches are primarily teachers who teach their sport and also teach values that help young adults grow into mature adults. While many coaches *are* teachers of both sport and values, many are not. Coaching is a job and coaches want to keep their jobs. Many coaches simply try to recruit the best players, use them to win as many games as possible, and thereby make their jobs as easy—and secure—as possible. Winning improves the coach's job stability, helps the coach ensure a more lucrative contract, and also helps the coach enhance opportunities for outside income (from shoe companies, on the lecture circuit, or running camps).

If your coach is the coach who recruited you, chances are he/she is going to give you every opportunity to succeed or fail. A coach doesn't want to look like a bad recruiter. But in order to get the fairest shake possible from this coach and maximize your opportunities to play and excel, you must:

- *Have open communication.* Let the coach know what your hopes and goals are for yourself and the team and learn what the coach's goals are. Ask the coach how he/she feels about contact from your parents or guardian. Some coaches are pleased to talk to parental figures, but others see parents as an imposition. Coaches do not like to have to justify their decisions to anyone, but they especially don't like having to justify their decisions to parents, since parents— no matter how team-oriented—always have one player's interests, your interests, foremost in their minds.

● *Work consistently hard year-round and especially at practice.* Let your coach see how badly you want to play, play well, and win. Even if you're not the greatest athlete, a great work ethic will always win you favor with a coach.

● *Develop a relationship with the assistant coaches.* Sometimes a head coach is too busy to always deal with you and you're going to want someone else to talk to and trust. Also, assistant coaches can generally spend more time working with you after practice if you want to improve a specific technique or skill. Although assistant coaches are generally extremely loyal to the head coach's philosophies, an assistant might be willing to offer you a different perspective on a strategy or principle or explain what a head coach may be trying to accomplish in a better way than the head coach can. By bringing any problems to a trusted assistant first, that assistant may be able to (1) act as a buffer between you and the head coach, (2) prepare you to better communicate your problems to the head coach, or (3) respond to your problems so you don't have to go to the head coach and risk a potentially hostile relationship.

● *Take an interest in the coach's family.* This doesn't mean you have to baby-sit the coach's kid when he wants to go the movies, it means that you should make occasional small talk ("How's your wife/husband?" etc.) to let the coach know that you realize he's a person with a life beyond your sport. If the coach's spouse, children, or parents attend games, always try to say hello and *always* be courteous.

● *Express admiration for the coach (indirectly).* If you frequently tell your coach what a great job he/she's doing, your coach is going to become suspicious of your motives and sincerity and your teammates are going to label you a suck-up. If you think your coach is doing a great job, be positive in other ways: Tell a coworker in the athletic department or mention it to your academic adviser. Word will filter back. And even if the kind words are not directly attributed to you, you'll be helping to enhance a good coach's reputation.

● *Express complaints about your coach carefully.* If you're having problems relating to your coach and you're confident that you've made every effort to resolve the situation but things are still not going your way and you're sure you don't want to transfer, you must be very careful to whom you complain because you may get yourself into a doghouse you will never dig your way out of. Continue to talk to the coach if you feel you're getting a raw deal. Do not confront the coach in public and do not swear or get excited. Discuss your situation and frustrations as rationally and calmly as you can and try to get definitive answers to your questions. Do not let your coach stonewall you.

If you're doing something wrong, or the coach doesn't like your personality or you're not in the coach's plans, you need to know so you can make an informed decision about quitting the team and concentrating on your academics or transferring to another school where you might—emphasize *might*—be more appreciated. Keep in mind that the grass isn't always greener on the other side and problems that plague you at your present school may plague you at a new school.

Transferring

Transferring has become epidemic because so many student athletes are making poor decisions coming out of high school. You should only transfer if you feel confident that you were misled or misguided when making your first decision, or if your thought processes were messed up when you made your decision, or the coach has changed *and* the new coach has brought in a new philosophy that you don't subscribe to or has plans that will leave you out in the cold. If you feel you were sold a bill of goods, you must confront the coach. If you feel you are being recruited over, you need to find out why.

But even taking all these considerations into account, you must also weigh your feelings about the school overall. If you have made a lot of friends and like your classes and professors, then you probably shouldn't transfer. The only time you should transfer solely for athletic reasons is when you are not getting a chance to play (and playing is *that* important to you) or you feel that your chances of making it as a professional are being severely hindered by your situation. And you have to be honest here. If you're not starting for one team, you'll probably not start for another team at the same level—but you could be a star if you play for a lower-ranked program in a smaller conference. Don't kid yourself. You may have already done that the first time, sucking up to the celebrity and having your ego fed by people who don't really care about you. And look where it got you. Now you want to leave.

Dealing with Your Teammates

Whether you participate in a team sport (football, basketball, baseball, soccer) or as an individual (golf, tennis, fencing, gymnastics), you are going to have teammates. And while being best pals with them isn't necessarily essential, for the sake of team chemistry, you're going to have to get along. Fortunately, this isn't a problem on most college teams because teammates often share common character traits: a love of the sport, a desire to improve, and a will to win. These three factors frequently smooth over any differences that the individuals might have regarding their backgrounds or interests.

Still, dealing with your college teammates will be more challenging than dealing with your high school teammates for several reasons:

● *The stakes are higher and the rewards are greater.* Millions of dollars can ride on the success of your college team. National championships and professional contracts might be at stake. That leads to . . .

● *More pressure.* People of all ages react differently, often oddly, under pressure. And just as some teammates will perform at their best when they face big-game pressure, others will fade. Knowing how your teammates (and coaches) respond to these higher stakes and game pressures will play a major part in your team's success. Knowing how your teammates (and coaches) respond to pressure (pregame, postgame, and in between games) will play a major role in how well all of you get along.

"Pressure is hard," says former NBA star Tom McMillen. "Some kids can handle it and some kids can't. I didn't have anything magical. I just got caught up in the excitement of the game. But one thing that kids can do is try to practice under pressure. There's no easy answer to it, but practice is the best way to deal with pressure. If you shoot a foul shot enough times, then you'll feel comfortable doing it in the middle of a game. If you don't, you won't."

● *The egos are bigger.* Most of your teammates will be equal to or better than the best of the best you played against in high school. They are accustomed to success. They are accustomed to being stars.

● *You spend more time together.* In high school you had a separate life away from school. In college, you don't. And while you can avoid a teammate who rubs you the wrong way when you're away from the team, you still have to practice together and travel together and attend team functions together. Depending on the living situation at the school you choose, you may even have to live together.

• • • •

Key #1: Respect yourself. Respect your teammates.
The two concepts go hand in hand. If you don't have respect for yourself, you can't have respect for anyone else. If you don't respect anyone else, there's no chance that anyone else will respect you. Thus, a vicious cycle.

• • • •

The real reason colleges have psychology departments is so that athletes can take the courses and learn how to relate to their teammates (and coaches, for that matter). Understanding what makes your teammates tick and what sets them off will go a long way toward making your relationships pleasant ones. *Examples:* Some teammates can take a little needling, others can't. Some teammates only want to get tips from the coaches. Others are willing to listen to what their fellow athletes have to say. Some teammates want to hang out with their teammates every minute of the day and others want to go off and be by themselves.

Understanding the wants and needs of your teammates is part of giving yourself a *psychological edge.* Most young athletes believe that if they have a psychological edge over their opponents that's enough. But in practice, your teammates *are* your opponents—two ways. First, you are competing against your teammates for playing time, roles, and so on. You are also competing against your teammates when you divide up and play against each other—or are asked to mimic the game plan of an upcoming opponent. Knowing how to play against your teammates, yet still be supportive of them, takes a great deal of psychological skill.

Psychology is also important in trying to get your teammates to put aside their egos to work with you for the good of the team. Often this means that you have to tell your teammates what they want to hear whether it is true or not. Stroke their egos when necessary. Avoid arguments at all costs. Your edge should be the ability to out-smart a teammate when his/her ego becomes an issue.

· · · ·

Key #2: Don't take things personally.

Until you spend a lot of quality time with people and make an attempt to understand why they are the way they are, you just have to take it for granted that not everyone behaves the way you behave. Sure, some upperclassman who you're trying to befriend may ice you, but it may have nothing to do with you or your personality. That athlete may feel that being seen with an underclassmen may hurt his/her image or your abilities may be seen as a threat. It's also possible that that athlete may be having trouble in class, at home, or with a boyfriend/girlfriend. Unless you make an effort to find out—and sometimes leaving well enough alone is the best option—you have no idea why the two of you aren't clicking. Maybe that teammate just isn't friendly. For all you know, he/she likes you better than he/she likes anyone.

· · · ·

The desire to succeed and the accompanying pressure (from coaches, relatives, friends, fans, alumni, the media) are often so great that some teammates will resort to any means necessary to get to, and stay at, the top. They'll freeze you out in practice. They'll backstab you to other players and coaches. Some of this they will do consciously and some will be done subconsciously. Occasionally, a teammate's ego is so big, he/she doesn't even realize he/she's bringing you down in order to build him or herself up. A good coach will see this happening and take steps, through communication, to correct it.

But many coaches don't spot the trends, and some coaches even help foster an environment of backstabbing and politicking, either wrongly equating it with competition or because they're misunderstanding—or choosing not to see—the signs. If a head coach is floundering and/or a team is losing, he may send out mixed signals to various players, thereby causing confusion and animosity. If there is a disagreement on a coaching staff over a style of play or a lineup change, one coach may build you up while another is bringing you down because he's building someone else up. Sometimes these moves are not done out of malice but out of legitimate differences of opinion over how best to coach a team. Or because the coaches don't communicate with each other.

That shouldn't matter to you. If you're being affected, you have to find out why. You have to be tough in practice. You have to talk— really talk, not pay lip service—to your coaches and your teammates. And you have to try to understand what's going on. You and everyone else on your team have to put ego aside enough to want what's best for the team, but you also have to make sure that you get a fair opportunity to learn and excel as an individual. If you're not good enough, that's one thing. If you're held back, that's another.

· · · ·

Key #3: Don't backstab.

What goes around comes around, and you don't want the people you work with, play with, and live with talking trash about you. You need to be the best you can be regardless of how anyone else behaves, and tearing down someone else only serves to reflect badly on you. A prize asset in a teammate is loyalty, so don't be shooting your mouth off.

Two other notes:

1 Any coach that will listen to and condone backstabbing of teammates and/or fellow coaches is a coach you have to watch out for. No two people in a competitive environment are *always* on the same page, but coaches should be supportive of each other and they have to be supportive of *all* their players. You're going to want your coach there for you if and when you need him, so be wary if you see him leave some other teammate out to dry.

2 Backstabbing is tattling, gossiping, or sniping. If you learn that a teammate has a problem with drugs, violence, gambling, or some other vice, informing someone in authority is not backstabbing. First, however, you should confront the teammate about his/her problem unless you believe that doing so could bring you potential harm. If you are close to that teammate, you can talk to him/her alone, but if you feel uncomfortable doing that you should ask other teammates (perhaps a captain) for support. When a teammate's problem has the potential to be bigger than the team, and bring the team down, it has to be dealt with.

· · · ·

When dealing with teammates it's important to know the player hierarchy and various cliques. Who are the leaders and who are the followers? Who are the gamers and who are the whiners? Who's friends with whom? Pick a role model from among the upperclassmen and try to follow the example that your role model sets. The captain is generally a good role model, but the captain may be too good athletically or may play a different position or may have too many demands on his/her time. Sometimes a teammate from the same hometown makes a good role model. The important thing is that you want to pick someone who

- sets a good example
- gets along with coaches and teammates

- has a good work ethic
- does well in school
- is patient
- is secure with his/her position on the team
- will give you the straight scoop on practices, road trips, teammates, opponents, and coaches
- will listen and offer advice when you have problems

Picking a good role model will go a long way to making your athletic experience more fun and rewarding.

• • • •

Competition for playing time *will* cause friction between you and your teammates, whether they're fighting you for a starting spot or they're the best friend of the player fighting you. This friction is to be expected. Let's face it, if you weren't competitive, you wouldn't be out there.

To lessen the friction, you have to communicate. Bring the issue of competition into daily, friendly discussion. It's okay to have different opinions in these talks (after all, you think you're better and he/she thinks he's/she's better), but it's important to keep your competition confined to athletics and not let it cloud your personal feelings for each other. Playing the same position on the same team at the same school, you and your teammates/rivals are going to have a lot in common. It's important that you support each other and help each other out whenever possible. It will help both you and the team in the long run. If, however, your overtures of support and friendship are refused, remain cordial and supportive. Knowing you are a bigger person will slowly eat away at your rival.

• • • •

Key #4: Be yourself.

You're unique as both an athlete and as a person. Be true to who you are and how you were raised. Don't get mixed up with a bad crowd because you think it will make you more popular. What will make you popular is treating people well and giving 100 percent in athletics and in the classroom. If you work hard and stay true to yourself, you'll sleep better and you'll perform better.

Learning to Live in the Public Eye
· ·

Athletes—even student athletes—are in the news a lot these days, and unless the coverage is for some on-the-field exploit, the publicity is generally bad. There seems to be another drug bust, assault, dorm room rape, or robbery involving an athlete almost every day, with the result being that an athlete with a promising collegiate or professional career suddenly finds himself suspended, expelled, or on the way to jail.

The reasons for this crime spree among athletes are many.

- A large number of student athletes come from crime-riddled neighborhoods and a few (and only a few) bad apples pick up the neighborhood's bad habits.
- Pampered for their entire lives because of their athletic ability, some student athletes feel they can do no wrong, that people will look the other way, that the coach will bail them out, and so on.
- What drives many great athletes is a great ego—they think they're invincible and they wrongly act as if they're invincible.
- Illegal performance-enhancing drugs change the athlete's brain chemistry and make him more violent than he otherwise might be.
- Pressure sometimes makes people do some awfully stupid things.
- Athletes are under a microscope, with fans and the media watching (and frequently taunting) their every move.

Too frequently, athletes use this last point as a crutch or cop-out: They're no different from anyone else, they say, they just got caught. Nonsense.

Athletes *are* different from everyone else: They're representatives of their university in the public arena, some are on a path to earn incredibly large sums of money based upon unique physical talents their nonathletic peers can only dream about, and (like it or not) they're in the public eye. When an athlete gets caught violating a team or NCAA policy—or worse, breaking the law—he not only hurts himself and his loved ones, but the college he represents, the coach he plays for, and the fans who look up to and cheer for him. And depending on the indiscretion, the punishment can last a lifetime.

It's not worth it.

If you're a student athlete who chooses to attend a small college away from the media's glare and play your sport at a relatively low-stress level, you won't have to worry too much about being in the public eye. But if you're talented enough to seek (and merit) the spotlight in a big-time sport at a big-time athletic program, you're going to have to mature quickly in order to meet the off-field challenges of an aggressive media, pushy alumni, and amazing pressure to win.

"An important thing to remember is that the public eye is so superficial," says Olympic basketball star Jennifer Azzi. "Anyone who puts any stock in it is crazy. You have to please yourself first and the people around you, but I don't think it's important to even think about being in the public eye. Sometimes it just happens and there's not a lot you can do about it, but you're not going to get too much out of it in terms of security."

"I was very conscious of how people perceived me," says former La Salle basketball player Craig Conlin. "I did not want to come off as being stuck-up and arrogant and not wanting to talk with people. I was very conscious of trying to be friendly to everybody, shake hands, and just be pleasant and nice to people. Treat them the way that I would want them to treat me."

Here are a few tips about performing well in the public eye.

● *Keep a low-profile on campus.* Until you begin to feel comfortable with your college lifestyle, there's no reason for you to seek attention. Let your athletic accomplishments speak for you. Keep your mouth shut. Go to class. Do your work. Be polite. If you cop an attitude, people are going to be eager to see you fail.

● *Stay humble.* Nobody likes a giant ego. Sharing credit with others will make you popular with your teammates, coaches, and fans. In day-to-day relations with coaches, professors, and administrators, you will benefit more by asking questions and listening—really listening—to the answers as opposed to acting like an arrogant know-it-all.

Just try to keep in mind that you're only playing a sport. It's not like you're involved with World Peace, feeding the hungry, developing a cure for AIDS, or anything.

● *Increase your profile at high-publicity events.* When your team visits a hospital or schedules an alumni fund-raiser, try to make an impression. Taking a few minutes to play with a sick child can do wonders for the child's well-being and your own. Taking a few minutes to talk with an interested alum can only help your team's chances for support and your own job prospects down the road.

● *Improve your public speaking.* Some schools offer courses, but sometimes you will have to do this on your own. The benefits are enormous. No matter how smart an athlete is, if a reporter sticks a microphone in the athlete's face and the athlete comes across as ill-spoken and illiterate it reflects badly on the athlete, the team, and the school. Newspapers will frequently clean up your quotes (improving your grammar and removing crutch words such as "like" and "ya know"), but TV is not as forgiving. When you're on TV, you want to speak confidently and clearly—and for many of you that's going to take practice.

And wipe that sneer off your face. Smile once in a while. You're playing a game. You're having fun. And while smiling may not be cool on the streets and may wrongly imply weakness, when someone sticks a microphone in front of you, you're not on the streets. You're communicating. And you can either come across as a student athlete or a punk. Your choice.

Says Penn Relays director Dave Johnson: "When track and field became gradually professionalized in the 1980s, what was very clear in the process was that athletes realized that they were going to increase their marketability beyond just drawing appearance fees if they could talk. The greater and more consistent money involved public relations. They had to be able to think on their feet. What it came down to was communication. You need to be able to present yourself well. That is really the key. There is a need to understand other people and to be understood yourself."

● *On the road, behave "professionally."* When you travel with your team, you are an ambassador for your team, your school, and your city. Do not take advantage of your situation. Treat flight attendants, hotel clerks, and waitpersons as you would like to be treated. Do not be afraid to lead with your behavior. A team that conducts itself well on the road leaves a favorable impression wherever it goes.

• *Do not let fans get under your skin.* It doesn't matter whether you're a star or a benchwarmer, when you go on the road you're going to get booed, ridiculed, cursed at, and more. If you're a star, the treatment could be unmerciful because the opposing team's fans want to take you out of your game. If you're a deep sub, the fans may be unmerciful because they view you as an easy target. It shouldn't matter much either way because, as an athlete, you have to toughen yourself to rough treatment when you're away from home.

What's tougher to deal with as a player is when your own fans treat you badly. At the high school and college level, fans are generally supportive of their own players, but there are always some hostile, jealous, and inappropriate fans. All you can do, especially if you're trying as hard as you can, is try to not let it affect your game performance or off-court demeanor. Learn relaxation techniques from a guidance counselor or therapist. Try to turn the fans' negative reaction (at home or on the road) into a positive. Smile whenever possible to show that the pressure's not getting to you. Focus on your game and not on the crowd. Do not try to do things that you're not capable of in order to quiet the crowd. Don't snap at fans. And don't take your frustrations out on your coaches or teammates.

• *Do not let the media get under your skin.* The media can get under the skin of a young player a number of ways. Obviously, tough questions about individual or team performance can frustrate a student athlete. Having to answer questions about a coach or teammate in trouble or a scandal of some kind can also be unnerving. But for the player who's not accustomed to the increased media attention that being recruited or playing at college brings, the attention itself can cause anxiety.

"I think I handle the press and the media better than anybody," says 1996 NCAA woman's basketball player of the year Saudia Roundtree, "because once you get caught up in all that—in the hype, in the media—then you're finished. That may sound crazy but that's the way it is. If you get caught up in how good they say you are as opposed to how good you really are, then you're not going to reach your full potential. During my senior year I had so much media attention focused toward me, but you have to stay modest and you have to stay focused and give your teammates credit because without them there would be no me. You just have to keep your head on straight."

There's more, however, than how the media affects you. Another issue to deal with is how you affect the media. Being in the spotlight forces a student athlete to confront a possible public speaking fear and also be accountable in print for what he/she says in an interview.

"It's important to be able to develop a relationship with people who are writing about you," says Dave Johnson, who frequently reports on track and field. "Most times, reporters are fair. There are times, however, when people are misquoted or more likely feel they're misquoted because there's something missing in the nuance of what they were saying. You can say the same words but with an inflection in your voice that means you were being sarcastic and you may have a story blow up in your face because the reporter didn't understand that. You need to realize that what you're saying is going to be put into print and read. And what may be an off-the-cuff comment to someone else might be picked up by someone else in a pool of reporters and be taken out of context.

"The best way to get around that is to have some type of understanding of the people asking you questions and their business. Just because someone is asking you questions now doesn't mean they're not going to be back some time in the future. You should pay as much attention to them as they are to you. That may be impossible—there may be twenty people asking you a question and it may be the same dumb question from all twenty of them, but if you can gradually get to know who they are then you'll be on better footing."

Also note that reporters share quotes with each other. They run in packs. They don't want to be out on a limb by themselves. So watch what you say and don't leave yourself out on a limb where your words can be used against you by an opponent, a teammate, or your coach.

Networking with Alumni

For many of you, an alumnus may have been instrumental in your college choice—either as an adviser, booster, or family friend. For others, your first contact with alumni will come as a varsity athlete—either at a practice, a dinner, a get-to-know-the-players function, or in your coach's office.

Learning to relate to alumni can have tremendous positive benefits during and after your college career, so you should always do what you can to be cooperative and polite. You should also find out from your coach what is acceptable (by NCAA standards) in a relationship with an alumnus because you don't want some overeager booster to get you, your teammates, and your coach in trouble.

How can alumni support help you? Perhaps when you need a job or summer job (if one is allowable under your financial aid/scholarship situation), or when you and your team are looking to travel overseas as part of a recognized program and you need to raise money, or when you seek career advice or help choosing a career after college. Well-connected alumni might be able to get your foot in a door that might otherwise be closed or help you get through the door of a company executive who never talks to new hires.

Says Major Indoor lacrosse star Scott Gabrielsen: "Your alumni are probably your ace in the hole. If you know anything about sales, a 'warm' call is a lot better than a 'cold' call. If you can get a warm feeling from someone that you have a tie to, you've already opened a door for yourself and you've broken down the barriers of getting into a certain situation. Alumni, no matter where they went, are always proud of the alma mater, they're proud of the sport that they played, and anybody who is coming up through the same ranks that they did. They can look at this person and put themselves in his/her place—like, hey, I was a college kid just like them at one time and if I can help them out I'd be happy to. So I think the networking of alumni is almost critical with regard to getting into a school as well as getting a job upon graduation from college. Never be scared to throw out that you went to the same school as the person you're wishing to contact."

An alumnus might also be able to help you handle your personal finances, negotiate your contracts, invest for the future, and allow you to draw on his/her experiences and to help prepare you better for your own decisions. An alumnus, especially one who might have had similar academic or athletic experiences, might also turn out to be a friend.

"Networking with alumni is really important," says fencer Peter Cox. "When I first went to Penn State, we had the alumni come down, and one of the things I loved about the school was how close the fencers were to the fencers who had already graduated. Some of the alums actually became some of my best friends, talking to me, keeping in touch with me, telling me to talk to this professor, and if you're doing poorly in this class make sure you do this and this or consider doing extra credit. They give you little hints to help you do better and then afterwards, once you build those contacts, they're already out in the world and they can help open some doors as well as give you good advice on how to get started and continuing on with the next step of life."

As long as you don't allow an alumnus to take advantage of his/her status and financial situation in ways that are against the rules of the NCAA and your school, you should seek support from interested alumni because they enjoy helping—it's their way of giving something back to their school and ensuring that the program stays healthy and successful.

So at some points in your career—probably once during your freshman year and once during your senior year—sit down with your coach, talk about the career choices you're considering, and ask if there are any alumni whom he/she might recommend you speak with, then try to find out a bit about that person so you can carry on a conversation with him/her and not just seem like you have your hand out asking for a favor. Talking to alumni in this manner will also help acclimate you to talking to adults (other than your relatives) in a nonthreatening way since alumni are generally predisposed to helping you.

Craig Conlin says: "Try and meet as many people as you can in college and network yourself while you're there. As the saying goes, 'It's not what you know, it's who you know.' And it really seems to be true in the workforce. Rarely do you walk up to someone and ask them how they got their job and they say, 'Oh, I found it in the classifieds.' It's always 'I knew so-and-so' or 'My uncle knew so-and-so.' Everybody knows somebody. That's what I try to get across to my brothers and my players. Be friendly to everybody. Don't burn any bridges. It's a small world and anybody could help you out in the end—you never know. So network with alumni or anyone you come across; you never know who they know or who they are.

"Being on a team and in the public eye gave me a good opportunity to get in front of alumni groups and get to know certain types of people," Conlin adds, "as opposed to the guys just sitting in the library. These alumni then know your name and know who you are. It can be very helpful."

Handling Adversity

A critical part of a student athlete's life is how well he/she deals with adversity. Not so much the adversity of losing—that's a different issue pertaining to how competitive you are—but the adversity associated with trying to succeed in college as both a student and an athlete.

During his fencing career at Penn State, Peter Cox faced a great deal of adversity. He let academics get the better of him at the start of college and injuries took their toll at the end of college. But Cox fought through his problems and eventually helped turn his injury into a career as a chiropractor.

"My senior year I tore a muscle in my lower back," Cox says, "and they told me it was a sciatica with a blown disc and that I could never fence again. The way I handled that stuff is I decided what it was that I wanted. I wanted to become NCAA champion my senior year and I achieved that—but I had to sacrifice practice time and put in rehab time to strengthen those back muscles. Then in 1992, I blew it out again during training and that's when I found out about chiropractic."

But physical pain wasn't all Cox had to endure. "Two years before the Olympics my youngest brother died in the middle of training, and that was a big shock and a big blow, but I still continued to move up in the ranks from number seven to number four even with that tragedy. Then, while I was training for the 1996 Olympics, my coach decided to leave me in the last year before the team selection. I needed somebody else to get me ready, but there was no one else in Kansas City [where Cox was attending Cleveland Chiropractic College] to fence with. So I asked my brother if he would work with me—he and I had fenced at Penn State for two years together—and he took me from number four to number one.

"You can have tremendous setbacks, but it depends how you want to view them, how you want to deal with them. You've got to be honest with yourself and let yourself know where you stand all the time. When I tried to make the Olympic team nobody gave me any support outside of my family and friends. The governing bodies said it's not gonna happen, you can't do it, but I did it."

Here are some of the other adverse situations you may be forced to deal with during your college career.

Academic Probation

Academic probation is a warning that indicates substandard academic performance—usually a GPA below 2.0. Academic performance is evaluated, at most schools, every semester. If a student athlete's GPA is below a 2.0, he/she will receive a conditional letter from his school. While on probation, the student athlete must raise the average above a 2.0 or face serious action—removal from the team or possibly expulsion. One of the reasons it's important to get off to a good start is because if you don't get a grip on your academic troubles early, it becomes more and more difficult to raise your cumulative average.

Although the NCAA has standardized rules about grade performance and eligibility, some athletic conferences—including the Ivy League and the Big 10—have adapted those rules to fit their own requirements. It is important to know what your school's policies are— specifically, how much slack they'll cut you academically during the season, when during the year eligibility decisions are made, how in-completes affect eligibility, and how summer school affects eligibility. In cases of academic probation and possible problems with eligibility, it is essential to have a coach who will go to bat for you and who is re-spected by your school's academic community.

The best way to deal with academic probation is to stay off it. Academic probation is caused by insufficient or inefficient studying time, a lack of course prerequisites, excessive socializing, misinter-preting what a professor expects, and not fully utilizing available re-sources.

Getting a letter placing you on academic probation is like going to overtime in a tie game. The pressure is on you to succeed, but if you put in the effort and do your best, you can still win.

Athletic Probation

Although it is possible for an individual player to be put on athletic probation, we are using the term with regard to team suspension. The way coaches and colleges are breaking rules these days, it seems as if some school or program is always going on NCAA-induced ath-letic probation. Probation is a serious, long-term suspension (usually lasting a year or two and hindering recruiting and/or TV appearances and/or postseason appearances) which can devastate the aspirations of student athletes, coaches, and university administrators.

If your school is hit with NCAA sanctions, however, you will be faced with a major decision. Is it wise to transfer, sit it out, or weather the storm until sanctions are lifted? The best thing to do, once again, is avoid the problem. Learn about the coach and school you're going to play for, make sure there are no investigations under way when you're making your decision, and make sure the coach is not commit-ting any recruiting violations during your own recruitment. If it's hap-pening to you, it's probably happened to someone else.

If, however, sanctions are placed on your team and/or your school, try to look at the big picture. If you have professional aspira-tions and you need to impress pro scouts, you may need to transfer. If you're an underclassman looking to make a name for yourself and see how good you can be, you may want to transfer. But if you're an upperclassman with no professional aspirations, you might as well stay where you are. The key thing to pay attention to is how much you enjoy school and how much of a pain it would be to have to start over again somewhere else.

Coaching Changes

It's a common problem: You agree to play for coach so-and-so and coach so-and-so decides to take another job. Or you build up a relationship with your coach and he/she gets fired. Coaching changes occur frequently at the collegiate level, and no one is more affected than the student athlete. After all, many of the athlete's collegiate and professional dreams revolve around the coach. If the student athlete wants to do all he/she can to ensure that the coach will be there for four years, the following steps are useful: (1) ask the coach what his/her plans and goals are; (2) find out the coach's job history (Is the coach stable? Does the coach move around a lot? Is the coach under a lot of departmental, alumni and media pressure?); and (3) find out if the coach's name comes up every time there's a job opening elsewhere.

Of course, none of these answers will ensure that the coach won't jump ship for the right offer, and student athletes must be mature enough to understand that the coach is just trying to advance his/her career. The bigger problem for the student athlete is when the coach is forced out. Whether it's deserved or not, when a coach is fired or forced to resign it throws a team into turmoil: the players feel a lot of stress (whether they like the coach and are trying to save his/her job or whether they dislike him/her and are playing under duress), the media coverage becomes more intense, and a sense of insecurity abounds.

When a school goes looking for a new coach, the players usually have very little say. They have no idea if their interests will be well-represented, they have no idea how they'll fit into the new coach's plans and style of play, and they'll have to learn a whole new set of communication skills. Some coaches talk the talk and others don't.

The key to success with a new coach is patience. The coach is also feeling things out, and everything he/she might know about you comes secondhand. If you had problems with the previous coach, or frequently mouthed off to the press or the administration, the new coach will probably be wary. The important thing is to really make an effort to communicate with the new coach, see where you stand, then try to approach things with an open mind. You, your new coach, and your teammates all must work together if you're to be successful.

Avoiding Injuries

Injuries can sap your talent or end your athletic career so it is very important that you take care of your body and get proper diagnosis and treatment when it is needed.

To help your body avoid injury:

- Make sure you are strong enough to compete at the level in which you're competing.
- Make sure your muscles are warm and stretched before any and all competition.
- Don't do stupid things like punch walls.
- Don't perform daredevil stunts.
- Don't party (or even exercise) to exhaustion.
- Eat well.
- Get enough rest.

Should you get injured, however, make sure you do not do anything to aggravate the injury or risk further injury. Here are some key steps to take to help you rebound from an injury.

- Seek prompt medical attention.
- Follow the doctor's instructions.
- Keep a positive frame of mind.
- Do not shortchange any rehabilitation.
- Do not try to come back from your injury before your body and your doctor say you're ready.
- If the injury does not heal as quickly as you hope, talk to your coach about the possibility of redshirting.

Olympic women's basketball star **Nikki McCray** came back from one of sports' most damaging injuries, a torn anterior cruciate ligament (ACL). "You have to be very strong to come back from an injury," McCray says. "But I had people that were very positive—my coaching staff, my teammates—and they really helped me a lot through the injury. Most important, you've got to set goals every day, stay very positive and very confident. I learned a lot about myself because of my injury. I've got more confidence and I'm more mentally tough."

 # Life after College

your college athletic career is done and you're on the verge of receiving that sheepskin you've worked so hard for. Now what? If you have dreams of a professional sports career, you've got to prepare yourself every way possible for that long-shot jump to the next level. If you're like everybody else, you have to find a job or move on to graduate school. We'll tackle these more typical concerns first.

Preparing to Make the Transition to the "Real World"

You faced a big transition when you moved from high school to college and you have a big transition ahead of you now. As you move from beyond the structured, insular framework of collegiate life, you will have a number of important questions to answer.

What Do You Want to Do?

It's a bit late to start thinking about what you want to do once you've received your diploma, but that is exactly when it dawns on a lot of student athletes that they have no prospects of a professional sports career and no more games to play. Having been catered to throughout their entire lives, they have incorrectly assumed that this arrangement would continue forever. It doesn't. Once your college athletic career is over you will often find former friends and advisers suddenly unable to return your phone calls.

That doesn't mean that all of your contacts just want to use you during your college career, it's just a warning that as an adult you have to be prepared to fend for yourself. For while it's important to network during your college years to help you determine a career option and meet people who can help make that option a reality, in the end a lot of it will come down to you—your ability, your maturity, your perseverance.

It is important that you therefore take every opportunity you can to get counsel from adults whom you respect about opportunities after college. Do you want to go into the sciences? Law? Politics? Retail? Sales? Or teaching? Have you always wanted to be a firefighter, a police officer, a stockbroker, or a writer? Use your coach and your coach's contacts to help you get in touch with professionals whom you would like to talk to and pump them for information. Find out requirements for various jobs. Starting salaries. What employment opportunities in entry-level positions are like.

If you're interested in a career that requires a graduate degree, make sure you have met with your academic adviser often enough so that your transcript is solid and you have taken the proper courses for admission. Work with this adviser to get you into the best possible graduate program in the field of your choice and make sure you, your adviser, and your parents and/or guardians explore every possible financial aid option. If you think college was expensive, wait until you decide to go to medical school.

If joining the family business is an option, talk it over with your parents or other relatives in the business and make sure that it is something you want to do and that they really want you involved. This conversation may get a bit uncomfortable, but it's better to discuss any concerns you might have at the beginning instead of keeping it all inside and ending up in the middle of an ugly family crisis a few years down the road.

As for help in deciding on and starting a career, employment expert **Carl Robbins** offers some advice. Robbins played basketball at the University of Pennsylvania 25 years ago and turned his Ivy League degree and an M.B.A. from the Wharton School into a career in human resources at companies such as Sperry, Towers-Perrin, and now Vanguard. Over the last 7 years, Robbins has specialized in corporate recruitment in particular, especially in the area of minority recruiting. Robbins says that student athletes bring some inherent weaknesses to the job market due to the tremendous amount of time they've spent playing their sport. But they also bring some strengths that the nonathlete can't bring to the table. It's important to play to your strengths.

When you're preparing to enter the job market, the first thing you need to do, Robbins says, is to "look at your peers who are not athletes and understand that from a potential employer's point of view there isn't any distinction. A potential employer is looking to fill a position, and if you don't have what he needs in terms of technical competencies he will look elsewhere.

"But student athletes should be mindful of the kinds of skills they are acquiring by virtue of the world that they're in at the moment. There are certain things that their peers are not acquiring, which is a sense of focus, dedication, and perseverance. These are all qualities that are viewed very favorably in the current labor market, where the drive these days is to try to evaluate candidates on behavioral tendencies instead of relying solely and exclusively on the cume. This is forcing a trend away from academic prowess to those behavioral traits that the interviewers must rely on. I would therefore say to the student athlete: 'Don't discount the technical acumen that your peers are acquiring but also don't discount the behavioral traits that are highly marketable that you might have by a function of your participation within the athletic program. These traits are indeed compensable in the labor market.'

"The disadvantage that the student athlete has," say Robbins, "is that from the point of view of employer contact, internships, or part-time jobs, their peers are getting a little bit of a leg up, and in the final analysis familiarity does have an advantage. To that end, the student athlete does lose a little bit because they don't have the time to do that. However, they can compensate for this disadvantage because the limelight that they're in makes it easier for them to get access by virtue of their success or visibility.

"Networking can therefore be very, very beneficial because there could be an opportunity that results from that activity. Secondly, you develop skill sets just like you're out there shooting foul shots—you can be out there practicing interviewing skills. And to that end, the people you network with are people who are inclined to help you. Now that should be a benefit, but it can also be a detriment because someone predisposed to help you may not be as critical in the screening process and may not be willing to offer back constructive criticism."

One last place to improve your marketability, says Robbins, is with the media. "There is a marginal benefit with the press," he says, "at least in terms of the reporters that I remember. They recognize that this is a group of amateurs and generally treat them with kid gloves, as distinct from, say, the professional players, who are free game. The student athlete should approach the interview session with a reporter as a time to practice skills. In that way they have lifelong benefits. But in terms of sticking your foot in your mouth, be careful."

The key, says Robbins, is to put yourself into this career mind-set early—in your sophomore year—and not wait until you've finished your senior year. "Understand your limitations and understand what you're bringing to the exchange," he says. "You're selling potential— the potential to fit in *and* do the job."

One of the ways Robbins is helping ballplayers at his alma mater realize their potential is through a unique, and newly designed, Mentoring Program drawing upon his years of experience. The Mentoring Program, which calls upon alumni and friends for everything from job contacts, to tips on résumé writing, interviewing, and dressing for success," came about because Robbins felt that student athletes were not recognizing their strengths and were not as polished as some of the nonathletic applicants they were competing against for jobs.

"I have vivid memories of reaching the end of my senior year and thinking I have no idea what I'm going to do. The extent of my career counseling to that point was to see someone in the placement office in March or April of my senior year. I think that that's wrong. You should be doing that earlier in your career and somebody should be prompting to you to do that.

"The problem is that you can't just rely upon the goodness of the coach, because I think a coach is not focused to deliver that type of advice and counsel. That's not how they're compensated. It's win or lose and if they lose, they're gone. Coaches don't have the time to shepherd students.

"I'm also not sure that coaches know how to prepare students for careers outside of their sport. There may even be a conflict of interest with the coach from the point of view that all they know and what they're preaching is in terms of their sport, and then we want them to be able to switch gears and talk about the world outside of their sport. They may not be able to switch gears. They don't know. This is not an area of their expertise. Nor do they care to know. That's just not part of their domain. So from a point of view of expectations, I don't have a lot. What I would like to see is a more well-rounded, more realistic understanding of what the odds are for a career within the sport and a balanced presentation—if not from the coach, from *somebody*—to make sure that students know their career options and the odds against a professional career in sports. You don't want a student athlete to look back on his or her college career after four years and feel that they have been exploited."

Keep in mind that, especially in this day and age, you are not married to a career choice for life. People change occupations all the time. By taking one job, you might learn about another field you didn't even know existed. Or a few years from now, jobs might open up in areas that don't even exist today.

Where Do You Want to Live?

Here you have to consider many of the same factors that went into your choice of a college. What region of the country do you want to be in? What type of climate? Big city or small town? Near your hometown or as far away as possible? And if you've had some athletic success, will either returning home or staying in your college area provide you with extra employment opportunities?

You also may have a few other factors to consider.

● Does the area where you wish to live support an industry in which you wish to work? *Example:* If you want to design clothes, there are probably more opportunities in New York's Garment District than in most whole states. But if you want to raise cattle, Oklahoma probably is a better bet than Manhattan. Those are perhaps outrageous examples, but you get the idea. Some areas of the country—due to weather, terrain, tax breaks, cheap real estate, or the desire for all top companies in a specific field to be near each other—are very strong in some areas and very weak in others. Do some research. Also check out what local taxes are like because you will find that a meager starting salary may actually be a fair wage in some places—money goes a lot farther some places than others.

● If you have a significant other, are engaged, or have a family, will you both be happy in your new environment? Will you both be able to find work? When your living arrangements are tied to another person (or persons), they automatically become more complicated. You don't want to be off at work all day and leave a spouse alone in an area where she/he feels uncomfortable or out of place. And if you have children, or expect to soon, you also may need to consider day care and school options.

How Will You Survive Financially?

This is an important one. For many of you, your first months after college will be the first time you have *all* the responsibilities of living on your own—including signing leases, commuting to work, repaying student loans, paying taxes, rent, utilities, insurance, and all those other things "adults" do.

For many, you will find it nearly impossible to make ends meet. If you end up with an entry-level job in a big city, you may have to borrow to fund the new wardrobe you need to dress for work. If you are a graduate student, you may have to take a part-time job or struggle to eat with a small student stipend.

It's therefore very important at the beginning of this transition to watch your money very carefully. Eating lunch out with your coworkers can get very expensive. Car payments and even bus fare can add up in a hurry. Try to make an income and expense chart (as detailed as possible) so you can track where your money goes.

If you're not too proud to ask, see if your parents or guardians can help you with financial support. Another option is to live at home for a while, until you can save some money.

Whatever you do, don't go crazy with credit cards. During your senior year, an endless parade of banks will try to sign you up for their credit cards. Getting a credit card can be an important step in building a credit history. But the key part of building a credit history is paying your bills. So don't overextend yourself. Eventually, you have to pay it all back.

Deciding Whether You're Good Enough to Play Professionally

If your sport has a professional option and you believe you're good enough to have a professional career—or you at least want to give it a shot—you have your own set of concerns.

Are You Good Enough?

As we've said previously, this will usually be decided for you, based upon both your success at the collegiate level and your physical strength and body type. If an agent or professional sports team believes you have the tools to succeed at the next level but just need some seasoning and skill refinement, they may take a chance on you.

Sports agent **Peter Roisman** represents golfers for Advantage International, a multisport agency with clients in basketball, football, tennis, swimming, and more. Roisman, whose advice can apply to all sports, says that "a fair indication of professional success is college success—although we have players who've won on the PGA tour, for instance, who never won a college golf tournament. There are various ways to get to being a successful professional, but most of it is the ability to work, the ability to compete, and the ability to stay in the game—financially staying alive while you have the ability and opportunity to improve."

The costs of attempting to establish a professional career, especially in sports like golf and tennis in which individualized instruction and travel are so important, can be quite high. "It's very expensive to continue along the golf career development path," Roisman says. "In fact, once you get out on the PGA tour it costs you in the neighborhood of seventy-five thousand dollars a year to sustain yourself and probably half that number on the Nike Tour. But the Nike Tour (kind of like the CBA or Triple A or World League of Golf) can be a great training ground. We happen to recruit more out of the Nike Tour than we do out of colleges, because on the Nike Tour players have gone through the college experience and are on to another level of play, which is generally the first time they've played competitively as a professional. Playing for money is very different than playing for titles, and we think it's a better indicator of success on the regular PGA Tour."

How Long Should I Try to Make It as a Pro?

This is entirely up to you, but there are a few good rules of thumb: (1) until your agent gives up on you; (2) until you stop making forward progress toward your goal (either in terms of athletic improvement or the level of play you're competing at); (3) until you run out of money and can no longer support yourself; (4) until a job possibility comes your way that might have more positive and likely career implications; or (5) until it's no longer fun.

Should My Parents or Guardians Have Any Role?

If they care about you, of course. You might have convinced yourself that you can be a pro, but you may be the only one who believes it. Talk over the options and make sure you have some adult support when you meet with prospective agents. You didn't want a college coach to sell you a bill of goods and you don't want an agent representing you who isn't looking out for your best interests.

How Can I Make Sure a Bad Agent Doesn't Cost Me Any Eligibility?

There have been so many scandals recently involving unscrupulous agents that players have had their careers ruined in their attempt to get a little cash a little quicker than is allowed. According to Peter Roisman, these are the basic rules of agent/athlete recruitment in plain English (for more information check appendix A or contact the NCAA):

"An agency trying to recruit a student-athlete may not provide that student-athlete with anything of value that that agency would not normally provide to any student of that same institution. Examples: I can't go on campus and drive a recruit around campus because I wouldn't normally go around and drive someone across campus. I can't provide that recruit with a soda. These are the smaller examples. I obviously can't send a plane ticket. If I were to have lunch with a recruit I would have to pay for myself and the recruit would have to pay for himself or herself.

"We can really stub our toe if we hurt an athlete's eligibility. It's the worst thing that can possibly happen. If we hurt the athlete we hurt ourselves in the process and everybody loses."

How Do I Pick an Agent?

"I'd choose an agent much like I'd choose a school," says Roisman. "I'd look for an agency that's had success and stability. I would look for an agency that has a good reputation in the way that it deals with not only its players but also the other members of the industry. In golf, for example, that would mean the equipment manufacturers, the tournament sponsors, and the tour itself. You probably should look for an agency that has broad scope in terms of its reach and its ability to deliver business opportunities for players. I would look for an agency that has a similar philosophy to me as a person in terms of how aggressively I would want to be represented. That's an important match and there has to be a comfort level there. And if I were choosing I would want a worldwide agency, but that's obviously something that not all agencies can offer."

"I think there's a right fit for everyone," says **Jeff Moorad,** partner in the firm of Steinberg & Moorad, which represents athletes like Troy Aikman, Steve Young, Drew Bledsoe, Will Clark, and Matt Williams. "At least, I like to think there is. Leigh Steinberg and I run a law practice that focuses on top players in football, baseball, and basketball and we work with two or three players chosen in the first round of those drafts each year. We rely heavily on referrals and recommendations rather than cold calls to prospective clients. That's a bit nontraditional in the industry, as the top player in any of those sports will receive one hundred to one hundred fifty unsolicited calls from people interested in representing them. We have found, though, that the referrals and recommendations produce a more ideal client relationship for the long term in our practice. We focus on a long-term sense of an athlete serving as a role model, retracing his routes and giving back to the communities that have supported him over time. And that philosophy isn't appropriate for every situation, but the types of players that call us are more interested in standing out off the field in a way that makes our practice attractive to them.

"Many agencies and firms involved in representing players will focus on second career opportunities. For example, in the financial advising area, an area that we're not directly involved in in our firm, we spend an inordinate amount of time helping a player choose an adviser in that arena and try to educate the player beyond the typical athlete level of sophistication so that he can understand his financial affairs and become proficient at overseeing those for the rest of his life."

· · · ·

Finding the right agent, however, will only be an issue for a very small number of you. Most of you will look back on your athletic experiences from other fields—with either fond memories, unfulfilled dreams, or a combination of the two. The important thing is to be able to look back and feel as if you got as much out of your abilities and set yourself as well as possible, in terms of life skills and contacts, for the time when your athletic career ends. The rest of your life now beckons. Make wise decisions and enjoy it.

The NCAA Guide for the College-Bound Student-Athlete

Reprint permission granted by the NCAA. This material is subject to change. For updates, call the NCAA at 1-913-339-1906.

THE NATIONAL COLLEGIATE ATHLETIC ASSOCIATION
6201 College Boulevard
Overland Park, Kansas 66211–2422
913-339-1906
NCAA Hotline: 800-638-3731
http://www.ncaa.org
April 1997

Text Prepared By: Stacey F. Herman, *Legislative Assistant*
Edited By: Michael V. Earle, *Director of Publishing*

Distributed to: Athletics Directors (Division I ADs receive 50; Division II ADs receive 40; Division III ADs receive 20), affiliated members and conference commissioners receive 20, corresponding members receive one.

NCAA, NCAA seal, NCAA logo and NATIONAL COLLEGIATE ATHLETIC ASSOCIATION are registered marks of the Association and use in any manner is prohibited unless prior approval is obtained from the Association.

Introduction

You're at an age when the last thing you probably want is more advice. But there's only one thing to do with good advice—pass it on.

As executive director of the NCAA, the best advice I can pass along if you plan to compete athletically at the college level is to start asking questions.

Find out if you're on track to meet academic eligibility and core-course requirements. See what the graduation rate of the athletics programs and the athletes in your sport are at the colleges in which you are interested. Ask what academic support services are available and how academic progress is tracked.

You'll notice that not one of those questions deals with the athletics side of being a student-athlete. Instead of focusing on which college can lead to a career in the pros, consider that:

● There are nearly one million high-school football players and about 500,000 basketball players. Of that number, about 150 make it to the NFL and about 50 make an NBA team.

● Less than three percent of college seniors will play one year in professional basketball.

● The odds of a high-school football player making it to the pros at all—let alone having a career—are about 6,000 to 1: the odds for a high-school basketball player—10,000 to 1.

Take a hard look at those numbers and think about what will matter in the long run—a college education.

There's another question you probably have: What is the NCAA?

The Association was founded in 1906. It is made up of 902 schools classified in three divisions (Division I has 305 schools; Division II has 246; and Division III has 351). Schools in Division I, which is divided into two divisions for football (Divisions I-A and I-AA), compete at the so-called major-college level.

The NCAA sponsors 81 championships in 22 sports. Almost 22,000 men and women student-athletes annually compete for NCAA titles.

Unfortunately, you occasionally hear about NCAA schools being put on probation for violating rules the colleges themselves have adopted.

This guide is intended to help you and your family understand these rules, which sometimes can be complex. If you have questions, contact our legislative services staff.

Choosing a college is difficult. Choose wisely to take that first step down the road to success.

—CEDRIC W. DEMPSEY
NCAA Executive Director

Academic Eligibility

"Recentered" SAT Scores

Please note that beginning with the April 1995 administration of the SAT test, SAT scores were "recentered" to a new scale. This new scale **does not** make the SAT test a more difficult test. It is a way for SAT to better justify its scoring system. As a result, the SAT scores used to meet NCAA initial-eligibility requirements changed. As indicated in the following sections, if you took the SAT on or after April 1, 1995, you are required to have a minimum test score of 820. Again, this will not change the level of difficulty of the SAT. For more information, please contact the NCAA legislative services staff at the address on page 189.

Division I Academic Eligibility Requirements

If you're first entering a Division I college on or after August 1, 1996, or thereafter, in order to be considered a "qualifier," you're required to:

● Graduate from high school

● Successfully complete a core curriculum of at least 13 academic courses [this core curriculum includes at least four years in English, two in math, one year of algebra and one year of geometry (or one year of a higher-level math course for which geometry is a prerequisite), two in social science, two in natural or physical science (including at least one laboratory class, if offered by your high school); one additional course in English, math or natural or physical science; and two additional academic courses (which may be taken from the already-mentioned categories, e.g., foreign language, computer science, philosophy)]

● Have a grade-point average (based on a maximum of 4.000) and a combined score on the SAT verbal and math sections or a sum score on the ACT based on the following qualifier index scale

Core GPA	ACT[1] (new: sum of scores)	SAT (old scoring system)	SAT (new scoring system)
Qualifier Index			
		before April 1, 1995	on or after April 1, 1995
2.500 & above	68	700	820
2.475	69	710	830
2.450	70	720	840–850
2.425	70	730	860
2.400	71	740	860
2.375	72	750	870
2.350	73	760	880
2.325	74	770	890
2.300	75	780	900
2.275	76	790	910
2.250	77	800	920
2.225	78	810	930
2.200	79	820	940
2.175	80	830	950
2.150	80	840	960
2.125	81	850	960
2.100	82	860	970
2.075	83	870	980
2.050	84	880	990
2.025	85	890	1000
2.000	86	900	1010

[1]Previously, ACT score was calculated by averaging four scores. New standards are based on sum

A "partial qualifier" is eligible to practice with a team at its home facility and receive an athletics scholarship during his or her first year at a Division I school and then has three seasons of competition remaining.

A partial qualifier may earn a fourth year of competition, provided that at the beginning of the fifth academic year following the student-athlete's initial, full-time collegiate enrollment, the student-athlete has received a baccalaureate degree.

In order to be considered a "partial qualifier," you have not met the requirements for a qualifier but you're required to:

- Graduate from high school

● Present a grade-point average (based on a maximum of 4.000) and a combined score on the SAT verbal and math sections or a sum score on the ACT based on the following partial qualifier index scale

	Partial Qualifier Index		
Core GPA	ACT° (new: sum of scores)	SAT (old scoring system)	SAT (new scoring system)
2.750 & above	59	600	720
2.725	59	610	730
2.700	60	620	730
2.675	61	630	740–750
2.650	62	640	760
2.625	63	650	770
2.600	64	660	780
2.575	65	670	790
2.550	66	680	800
2.525	67	690	810

°Previously, ACT score was calculated by averaging four scores. New standards are based on sum of scores.

Division II Academic Eligibility Requirements

If you're first entering a Division II college on or after August 1, 1996, or thereafter, in order to be considered a "qualifier," you're required to:

● Graduate from high school

● Have a GPA of 2.000 (based on a maximum of 4.000) in a successfully completed core curriculum of at least 13 academic courses [this core curriculum includes three years in English, two in math, two in social science, two in natural or physical science (including at least one laboratory class, if offered by your high school) and two additional courses in English, math or natural or physical science; and two additional academic courses (which may be taken from the already-mentioned categories, e.g., foreign language, computer science, philosophy)]

● Have a combined score on the SAT verbal and math sections of 700 if taken before April 1, 1995, or 820 if taken on or after April 1, 1995, or a 68 sum score on the ACT

A "partial qualifier" is eligible to practice with a team at its home facility and receive an athletics scholarship during his or her first year at a Division II school.

In order to be considered a "partial qualifier," you have not met the requirements for a qualifier, but you're required to graduate from high school and meet one of the following requirements:

- Specified minimum SAT or ACT score, or

- Successful completion of a required core curriculum consisting of a minimum number of courses and a specified minimum grade-point average in the core curriculum

Details of these general requirements are contained in the following sections.

Definition of a Core Course

To meet the core-course requirement, a "core course" is defined as a recognized academic course (as opposed to a vocational or personal-services course) that offers fundamental instruction in a specific area of study. Courses taught below your high school's regular academic instructional level (e.g., remedial, special education or compensatory) can't be considered core courses regardless of the content of the courses. For courses taken during and before the 1986–87 academic year to be considered core courses, at least some instructional elements (as listed below) must be included. However, effective with courses taken during the 1987–88 academic year and thereafter, at least 75 percent of the course's instructional content must be in one or more of the required areas (as listed below) and "statistics," as referred to in the math section, must be advanced (algebra-based).

English—Core courses in English include instructional elements in grammar, vocabulary development, composition, literature, analytical reading or oral communication.

Math—Core courses in mathematics include instructional elements in algebra, geometry, trigonometry, statistics or calculus.

Social Science—Core courses in social science contain instructional elements in history, social science, economics, geography, psychology, sociology, government, political science or anthropology.

Natural or Physical Science (including at least one full unit of laboratory classes if offered by your high school)—Core courses in natural or physical science include instructional elements in biology, chemistry, physics, environmental science, physical science or earth science.

Additional Academic Courses—The remaining units of additional academic credit must be from courses in the above areas or foreign language, computer science, philosophy or nondoctrinal religion (e.g., comparative religion) courses.

Questions and Answers about Core-Course Requirements

Q *Can courses taken after my senior year help satisfy core-course requirements?*
At Division I colleges, generally only courses completed in grades 9 through 12 may be considered core courses. Courses taken after the completion of your eighth semester (i.e., summer school after your senior year) may not be used to satisfy core-course requirements.

A student diagnosed with a learning disability is permitted to use all core courses completed before initial full-time enrollment at a collegiate institution. Please contact the NCAA national office for additional information regarding accommodations for students with learning disabilities.

At Division II colleges, you're permitted to use all core courses completed before initial enrollment at a college as certified on your official transcript or by official correspondence.

Q *Is there a way for me to be immediately eligible in Division I if I didn't complete my core courses in the first eight semesters?*
At Division I institutions, if you repeat an entire regular term or academic year of high school, you may use appropriate courses taken during that term or year to fulfill the core-course requirements. However, if the repeated term or year occurs after graduation, the core courses you use must be taken at the high school from which you graduated, and your initial full-time college enrollment cannot occur until the next academic year. In Division I, it is not permissible to substitute the grades earned in postgraduate high-school work in place of grades attained before graduation.

Q Can courses taken in the eighth grade satisfy core-course requirements?
Eighth-grade courses cannot satisfy core-course requirements.

Q How is my core-course GPA calculated?
Your core-course grade-point average may be calculated using your 13 best grades from courses that meet the core-course distribution requirements. Additional core courses (beyond the 13 required) may be used to meet the core-course grade-point average if the distribution requirements are met.

Q How many different courses must I take to satisfy core-course requirements?
You must present 13 different courses in meeting the core-course requirements. A repeated course may be used only once. Further, you may use your best grade in the repeated course in calculating the core-course grade-point average.

Q What do I need to present if I am in a home-schooling program?
All prospective student-athletes who are home-schooled will need to have their core-course requirements analyzed by the NCAA Committee on Initial-Eligibility Waivers.

Q Can I count independent study courses in my core-course requirements?
No. Independent study or correspondence courses may not be used to satisfy core-course requirements.

Q Do pass-fail grades count?
Yes, courses awarded pass-fail grades may be used to satisfy core-curricular requirements. The NCAA Initial-Eligibility Clearinghouse shall assign the course the lowest passing grade at the high school, which could be a grade of "D."

Q Do I have to successfully complete the core courses used to satisfy the core-course GPA requirement?
Yes. Students entering a Division I or II college as freshmen in the fall of 1988 and thereafter must have satisfactorily completed

all courses used to satisfy core-curriculum requirements. Satisfactory completion is defined as a nonfailing grade (i.e., a grade of "D" or above).

Q   Can college courses count toward core-course requirements?
A college course can satisfy core-course requirements if it is accepted by your high school and the course

a   Would be accepted for any other student;
b   Is placed on your high-school transcript; and
c   Meets all other requirements for a core course.

Q   How are courses taken over two years counted?
A one-year course that is spread over a longer period of time (i.e., two years, three semesters) is considered as one course (e.g., elementary algebra).

Q   Do preparatory classes count?
No. Effective with the 1993–94 academic year, a course taken to prepare for the first course normally taken to fulfill the progression of core-course requirements (i.e., prealgebra) may not be used as a core course regardless of the course content.

Q   How are core courses determined?
The NCAA Initial-Eligibility Clearinghouse determines whether a course qualifies as a core course after receiving information provided by your high-school principal. All approved courses are listed on a 48-H confirmation form, which is mailed to your high school each year.

Q   What if I leave high school after my junior year to enter an early admissions program?
You may receive a waiver of the initial-eligibility requirements if you enter an early admissions program (open to students solely on the basis of outstanding academic performance and promise), provided that for the last four semesters in high school, you maintained a cumulative minimum grade-point average of 3.500 (based on a maximum of 4.000), ranked in the top 20 percent of

your class and met all other requirements for graduation from high school, and the only remaining deficiency is in the core-course area of English (i.e., lacking one year of English).

Q Can courses for the learning disabled or handicapped count?

High-school courses for the learning disabled or handicapped may be used to meet the core-course requirements if your principal submits a written statement to the NCAA indicating that students in such courses are expected to acquire the same knowledge as students in other core courses and that the same grading standards are employed.

Documentation that these conditions have been met must be provided to the NCAA national office for approval. Please contact the NCAA national office for information regarding accommodations available for students with learning disabilities.

Q Can studies in a foreign country help satisfy core-course requirements?

If you've completed a portion of your secondary studies in a foreign country, your academic record should be submitted to the NCAA national office for review by the foreign-student records consultants.

Grade Values

The grade values listed below are used in determining your grade-point average in the core courses:

A = 4 quality points	C = 2 quality points
B = 3 quality points	D = 1 quality point

To determine the core-course grade-point average, convert each grade earned (including all numerical grades) to this 4.000 scale on an individual course basis. Pluses or minuses may not receive greater or lesser quality points. Your high school's normal practice of weighting honors or advanced courses may be used to compute the quality points awarded and the cumulative grade-point average if a written statement verifying the grading policy accompanies your official grade transcript.

Test-Score Requirements

In Divisions I and II, you must achieve the minimum required SAT or ACT score before your first full-time college enrollment. Your test scores must be achieved under national testing conditions on a national testing date [i.e., no residual (campus) testing or regional testing dates]. National testing dates are:

SAT 1997–98	ACT 1997–98
October 4, 1997	October 25, 1997
November 1, 1997	December 13, 1997
December 6, 1997	February 7, 1998
January 24, 1998	April 4, 1998
March 28, 1998	June 13, 1998
May 2, 1998	
June 6, 1998	

Test-Score Interpretations

◆ All prospective student-athletes, including natives of foreign countries, must achieve the minimum required test score on a national testing date. Foreign prospective student-athletes should contact the appropriate testing agency for more information about registering to take the test on a national testing date.

◆ The following interpretations apply to the combination of test scores from more than one national testing date:

● If you take the SAT, the highest scores achieved on the verbal and math sections of the SAT from two different national testing dates may be combined in determining whether you have met the minimum test-score requirement. [Note: This includes combining converted subscores from the "recentered" and "non-recentered" versions of the SAT.]

● If you take the ACT, the highest scores achieved on the individual subtests from more than one national testing date may be combined in determining whether your sum score meets minimum test-score requirements.

◆ The following have been approved regarding the SAT and ACT test-score requirement for learning-disabled students:

● The student must register for the nonstandard testing as outlined by the testing service, which requires that the handicap or learning disability be diagnosed professionally and properly documented and confirmed.

● The procedures outlined by the testing service must be followed, and the individual(s) giving the test may not be a member of your high school's athletics department or an NCAA school's athletics department.

● The following records must be sent to the NCAA national office:

1 A copy of all records sent to the testing service to register for the test, including the professional diagnosis of the learning disability or handicap
2 A complete record of your SAT or ACT scores, and
3 A statement from the person(s) giving the test that he or she is not a member of the athletics department at a high school or NCAA school

● Please note that if you take a nonstandard ACT or SAT, you still must achieve the minimum required test score; however, the test doesn't have to be taken on a national testing date.

● Assuming proper documentation is received, the NCAA Academic Requirements Committee then may approve your completion of the test-score requirement.

Waiver of Bylaw 14.3 Requirements

Waivers of the initial-eligibility requirements may be granted based on evidence that demonstrates circumstances in which your overall academic record warrants a waiver. All requests for such a waiver must be initiated through an NCAA school that officially has accepted you for enrollment as a regular student or if acceptance is contingent on a favorable subcommittee decision. You should contact the school recruiting you for more information about this waiver process. Students with learning disabilities may initiate the initial-eligibility waiver process on their own without the help of a member institution. Please contact the national office for more information.

An exception also may be granted if you left high school after completion of your junior year or during your senior year to enter a Division I or II school under an early admissions program on the basis of outstanding academic performance and promise. To be granted this exception, you must have maintained an accumulative 3.500 GPA and must have ranked in the top 20 percent of your class for the last four semesters completed in high school. In addition, all requirements of a qualifier (core curriculum and test scores) must be met except graduation from high school and a fourth year of English.

Additional Information

Several additional points about the NCAA's initial-eligibility requirements should be emphasized:

● These requirements currently do not apply to Division III colleges, where eligibility for financial aid, practice and competition is governed by institutional, conference and other NCAA regulations.

● This rule sets a minimum standard only for athletics eligibility. It's not a guide to your qualifications for admission to college. Under NCAA rules, your admission is governed by the entrance requirements of each member school.

● The General Education Development (GED) test may be used under certain conditions to satisfy the graduation requirement of Bylaw 14.3 but not the core-course or test-score requirements. Contact the NCAA national office for information about these conditions.

Initial-Eligibility Clearinghouse

A central clearinghouse will certify your athletics eligibility for Divisions I and II. Here is some important information that will assist you.

Certification

If you intend to participate in Division I or II athletics as a freshman, you must register and be certified by the NCAA Initial-Eligibility Clearinghouse. Refer to pages 191 through 201 to determine the initial-eligibility standards that apply to you.

Clearinghouse Registration Materials

Your counselors can obtain registration materials, at no cost, by calling the clearinghouse at 319-337-1492.

Registration Process

Your counselors should provide you with a student-release form and a red brochure titled, "Making Sure You Are Eligible to Participate in College Sports." In order to be registered with the clearinghouse, you must complete the student-release form and mail the top (white) copy of the form to the clearinghouse along with the $18 registration fee. Give the yellow and pink copies of the form to a high-school official who then sends the yellow copy, along with an official copy of your high-school transcript, to the clearinghouse. Your high school should keep the pink copy for its files. After graduation and before the school closes for the summer, your school also must send the clearinghouse a copy of your final transcript that confirms graduation from high school.

Fee Waivers

High-school counselors may waive the clearinghouse fee if you have previously qualified for and received a waiver of the ACT or SAT fee. Fee-waiver information is specified on the student-release form.

Test Scores

To be certified, you also must submit your ACT or SAT scores to the clearinghouse. You may either have your scores sent directly from the testing agency to the clearinghouse or have your test scores reported on your official high-school transcript. You can have your scores sent directly to the clearinghouse by marking code 9999 as one of the institutions to receive your scores on your ACT or SAT registration form or by submitting a request for an "Additional Score Report" to the appropriate testing agency.

Form 48-H

Your high school must annually file one Form 48-H with the clearinghouse that lists your school's core courses that meet NCAA requirements. Without a Form 48-H for the current academic year, you cannot be certified as eligible. The 48-H confirmation form identifies only courses that may be used in meeting NCAA core-course requirements.

Be sure that all courses that you are taking for core-course purposes are listed on your high school's 48-H confirmation form.

Questions and Answers about the Clearinghouse

Q *Why do I need to register and be certified?*
If you intend to participate in Division I or II athletics as a freshman in college, you must be registered with and be certified as eligible by the NCAA Initial-Eligibility Clearinghouse. Refer to pages 191 through 201 to determine the initial-eligibility standards that apply to you. Please note that initial-eligibility certification pertains only to whether you meet the NCAA requirements for participation as a freshman in Division I or II athletics and has no bearing on your admission to a particular Division I or II institution.

Q *When should I register?*
You should register with the clearinghouse whenever you decide you would like to participate in athletics as a college freshman. It's generally best to register after your junior-year grades appear on your transcript. Although you can register anytime before participation, if you register late you may face delays that will prevent you from practicing and competing.

Q *How do I register?*
You will need to obtain registration materials from your high-school guidance counselor. (If your school has run out of materials,

your counselor should call the clearinghouse at 319-337-1492 to obtain additional forms.) These materials include a student-release form and a red brochure titled, "Making Sure You Are Eligible to Participate in College Sports." Fill out the student-release form completely and mail the top (white) copy of the form to the clearinghouse along with the $18 fee. (The fee can be waived if you received a waiver of the ACT or SAT fee.) Give the pink and yellow copies of the student-release form to your high-school counselor who will then send the yellow copy, along with an official copy of your high-school transcript, to the clearinghouse. The high school will keep the pink copy of the form for its files.

Q   What if I have attended more than one high school?
If you have attended multiple high schools since ninth grade, each school will need to send your official transcript to the clearinghouse. You should give the pink and yellow copies of the student-release form to the counselor at the high school from which you will be graduating. You also will need to make copies of this form and send them to the counselors at the other schools that you have attended.

Q   Are standardized test scores required?
Qualifying test scores are required for participation at both Division I and Division II colleges. If you intend to participate at either a Division I or II school, the test scores may be taken from your official high-school transcript.

Q   How can I arrange for my scores to be sent directly from the testing agency?
When you register to take the ACT or the SAT, you can mark code 9999 so that the clearinghouse will be one of the institutions receiving your scores; or alternatively, you can submit a request (and fee) for an "Additional Score Report" to the appropriate testing agency by indicating code 9999 on your request form.

Q   What will the clearinghouse provide to the colleges that are recruiting me?
The clearinghouse will send your eligibility status to any Division I or II college that requests it, provided you have given permis-

sion on your student-release form for the college to receive that information. Please note that the clearinghouse will not send your eligibility information at your request; rather, the college must make the request for that information.

Financial Aid

If you've met Bylaw 14.3 requirements and are enrolled in a Division I or II college, you may receive financial aid from the school that includes tuition and fees, room and board, and books.

In addition, student-athletes who haven't met Bylaw 14.3 requirements may receive financial aid under specified conditions.

In Division I, a "partial qualifier" (as defined on page 192) may receive an athletics scholarship. A "nonqualifier" (someone who has not met the requirements to be considered a "qualifier" or a "partial qualifier") in Division I may receive need-based financial aid unrelated to athletics.

In Division II, a "partial qualifier" (someone who has not met all Bylaw 14.3 requirements but who has graduated from high school and has fulfilled either the core-course or the standardized test-score requirement) may receive institutional financial aid, including athletically related financial aid.

In Division II, a nonqualifier (someone who has not met the requirement to be considered a "qualifier" or a "partial qualifier") may receive institutional financial aid unrelated to athletics ability.

There's no guaranteed four-year athletics scholarship in Division I, II or III. An athletics scholarship is awarded for one academic year. It may be renewed each year for a maximum of five years within a six-year period.

In some cases, you may receive additional financial aid, such as the Pell Grant, from government programs. Ask your college's financial aid office for more information about such aid.

If you receive a scholarship from your high school or local civic or booster club, tell your college recruiter so he or she can notify the school's financial aid office.

If you plan to attend a Division III college, you may receive financial aid up to the cost of attendance (tuition and fees, room and board, books, transportation, and other expenses incidental to attendance) if

the aid is based on financial need and not associated with athletics
ability.

Recruiting

You become a "prospective student-athlete" when you start ninth-
grade classes. Before the ninth grade, you become a prospective
student-athlete if a college gives you (or your relatives or friends) any
financial aid or other benefits that the college does not provide to
prospective students generally.

You become a "recruited prospective student-athlete" at a particular college if any coach or representative of the college's athletics
interests (booster or representative) approaches you (or any member
of your family) about enrolling and participating in athletics at that
college. Activities by coaches or boosters that cause you to become a
recruited prospective student-athlete are:

- Providing you with an official visit;

- Placing more than one telephone call to you or any other
member of your family; or

- Visiting you or any other member of your family anywhere
other than the college campus.

Division I

In addition to general recruiting regulations, no alumni, boosters, or
representatives of a college's athletics interests can be involved in
your recruiting. There can be no phone calls or letters from boosters.

The restriction doesn't apply to recruiting by alumni or representatives as part of a college's regular admissions program for all
prospective students, including nonathletes.

You (or your family) may not receive any benefit, inducement, or
arrangement such as cash, clothing, cars, improper expenses, transportation, gifts, or loans to encourage you to sign a National Letter of
Intent or attend an NCAA college.

Letters from coaches, faculty members and students (but not boosters) aren't permitted until September 1 at the beginning of your junior year.

Telephone Calls

In all sports other than football, phone calls from faculty members and coaches (but no boosters) are not permitted until July 1 after completion of your junior year. After this, in sports other than football, a college coach or faculty member is limited to one telephone call per week to you (or your parents or legal guardians), except that unlimited calls to you (or your parents or legal guardians) may be made under the following circumstances:

- During the five days immediately before your official visit by the college you will be visiting
- On the day of a coach's off-campus contact with you by that coach
- On the initial date for signing the National Letter of Intent in your sport through two days after the initial signing date

In football only (other than Division I-A), an institution's coaches may telephone you as often as they wish during a contact period (see page 209), but that telephone contact may not occur before August 15 after the completion of your junior year. Also, an institution's football coaches can telephone you as often as they wish during the period 48 hours before and 48 hours after 7 A.M. on the initial signing date for the National Letter of Intent. Outside of a contact period, a football coach may only telephone you once per week.

In Division I-A football, an institution's coaches may telephone a prospect once during the month of May of the prospect's junior year in high school and then not again until September 1 of the prospect's senior year in high school. In Division I ice hockey, an institution's coaches may telephone a prospect who is a resident of a foreign country once during the month of July following the completion of the prospect's sophomore year in high school.

You (or your parents) may telephone a coach at your expense as often as you wish.

Coaches also may accept collect calls from you and may use a toll-free (1–800) number to receive telephone calls from you on or after July 1 after completion of your junior year.

Enrolled student-athletes may not make recruiting telephone calls to you. Enrolled students (nonathletes) may telephone you as part of a college's regular admissions program directed at all prospective students. Enrolled students (including student-athletes) may receive telephone calls at your expense on or after July 1 after completion of your junior year.

Contacts

A college coach may contact you in person off the college campus only on or after July 1 after completion of your junior year. Any face-to-face meeting between a college coach and you or your parents, during which any of you says more than "hello" is a contact. Also, any face-to-face meeting that is prearranged or that occurs at your high school or competition or practice site is a contact, regardless of the conversation. These contacts are not permissible "bumps."

Currently in all sports other than football, coaches may contact you off the college campus no more than three times. However, a college coach may visit your high school (with the approval of your high-school principal) only once a week during a contact period.

Football coaches may contact you off the college campus seven times. However, no more than one contact per week may occur during a contact period (see page 209), regardless of where the contact occurs. Also, a college football coach may visit your high school (with the approval of your high-school principal) only once a week during a contact period.

In Division I ice hockey, coaches have seven recruiting opportunities (contacts and evaluations) during the academic year and not more than three of the seven opportunities may be in-person, off-campus contacts.

Evaluations

An evaluation is any off-campus activity used to assess your academic qualifications or athletics ability, including a visit to your high school (during which no contact occurs) or watching you practice or compete at any site.

Currently in all sports other than football and basketball, coaches may not evaluate you more than four times each academic year. Basketball coaches have five "recruiting opportunities" to utilize on you during any year. In using those five opportunities, a basketball coach may use any combination of contacts and/or evaluations that equal five; however, not more than three of the opportunities may be in-person contacts. Football coaches may not evaluate you more than two times each year (May 1 through April 30). In football, only one evaluation may be used during the fall evaluation period and only one evaluation may be used during the May evaluation period. In all sports, competition on consecutive days within a tournament (and normally at the same site) or that involves a tier of a tournament (e.g., regional) counts as a single evaluation. In addition, once you sign a National Letter of Intent, you may be evaluated an unlimited number of times by a college coach from the college with which you have signed.

In football and basketball only, there are certain periods (see below) when a coach may contact you off the college campus and/or attend your practices and games to evaluate your athletics ability. In all other sports, contacts and evaluations may occur anytime except during a dead period.

1997–98 Contact Periods

Football—December 1 through December 23, 1997; January 2 through January 3, 1998; January 9 through January 31, 1998.

Men's Basketball—September 9 through September 26, 1997; March 16 through March 22, 1998; April 1 (8 A.M.) through April 5, 1998; April 10 through April 15, 1998.

Women's Basketball—September 10 through September 29, 1997; March 1 through March 24, 1998 (a college has eight contact days to use at its discretion); March 30 (noon) through April 5, 1998.

1997–98 Evaluation Periods

Football—During any contact period; nine days during October and November 1997 (selected by the college); 20 days (excluding Memorial Day and Sundays) during May 1998 (selected by the college).

Men's Basketball—During any contact period; July 8 through July 31, 1997; November 20, 1997, through March 15, 1998 (40 evaluation days selected by the college); July 8 through July 31, 1998.

Women's Basketball—During any contact period; July 8 through July 31, 1997; October 8, 1997, through February 28, 1998 (40 evaluation days selected by the college); July 8 through July 31, 1998; during the National Junior College Athletic Association and Amateur Athletic Union national championships; during official tryouts for the USA Basketball Olympic Festival [Note: For states that play high-school basketball in the spring, April 8 through April 28 and July 8 through July 31; for Hawaii, March 1 through May 31 and July 8 through July 31].

[Note: There's a "dead" period (when coaches may not contact or evaluate you on or off the college campus) in all sports 48 hours before and 48 hours after 7 A.M. on the initial National Letter of Intent signing date.]

You may not try out for a Division I college's athletics team. A tryout is any physical activity (e.g., practice session or test) conducted by or arranged on behalf of the college, at which you display your athletics ability.

You can visit a college campus any time at your expense. On such a visit, you may receive three complimentary admissions to a game on that campus and a tour of off-campus practice and competition sites in your sport and other college facilities within 30 miles of the campus.

Official Visits

During your senior year, you can have one expense-paid (official) visit to a particular campus. You may receive no more than five such visits. This restriction applies even if you are being recruited in more than one sport. You can't have an official visit unless you have given the college your high-school (or college) academic transcript and a score from a PSAT, an SAT, a PACT Plus or an ACT taken on a national test date under national testing conditions. Your academic transcript may be a photocopy of your official high-school (or college) transcript. [Note: In this instance, the Division I school may use the services of the Initial-Eligibility Clearinghouse to validate your credentials.]

During your official visit (which may not exceed 48 hours), you may receive round-trip transportation between your home (or high school) and the campus, and you (and your parents) may receive meals, lodging and complimentary admissions to campus athletics events. A coach may only accompany you on your official visit when the transportation occurs by automobile and all transportation occurs within the 48-hour period. Meals provided to you (and/or your parents) on an official visit may be provided either on or off the institution's campus.

The complimentary admissions you receive may provide you seating only in the facility's general seating area. You may not be given special seating (e.g., press box, bench area). In addition, a student host may help you (and your family) become acquainted with campus life. The host may spend $30 per day to cover all costs of entertaining you (and your parents, legal guardians or spouse); however, the money can't be used to purchase souvenirs such as T-shirts or other college mementos. Additionally, during a campus visit, the school may provide you with a student-athlete handbook.

Printed Materials

A Division I college that is recruiting you may provide to you only the following printed materials on or after September 1 of your junior year:

● Official academic, admissions and student services publications and videotapes published by the college;

● General correspondence, including letters and college note cards (attachments to correspondence may include materials printed on plain white paper with black ink);

● Game programs (a college may only give you a program on an official or unofficial visit; colleges may not mail you a program);

● A media guide or recruiting brochure (but not both) in each sport;

● Any necessary preenrollment information about orientation, conditioning, academics, practice activities, as long as you have signed a National Letter of Intent or have been accepted for enrollment;

● One student-athlete handbook. (A college may only give you a handbook on an official or unofficial visit. Effective August 1, 1997, a college may mail you a handbook once you've signed a National Letter of Intent or been accepted for enrollment.)

● One wallet-size playing schedule card in each sport.

In addition, a Division I college may show you a highlight film/videotape, but may not send it to or leave it with you or your coach.

Finally, a Division I college also may provide you a questionnaire, camp brochure and educational information published by the NCAA (such as this guide) at any time.

Division II

In addition to general recruiting regulations, no alumni or representatives of a college's athletics interests (boosters or representatives) can be involved in off-campus recruiting; however, you may receive letters from boosters, faculty members, students and coaches on or after September 1 of your junior year. In all sports other than football, telephone calls from coaches, boosters and faculty members are permissible on or after July 1 after completion of your junior year. In Division II football, telephone calls may not begin before August 15 after your junior year.

After this, in sports other than football, a college coach or faculty member is limited to one telephone call per week to you (or your parents or legal guardians), except that unlimited calls to you (or your parents or legal guardians) may be made under the following circumstances:

● During the five days immediately before your official visit (by the college you'll be visiting);

● On the day of the coach's off-campus contact with you;

● On the initial date for signing the National Letter of Intent in your sport through the two days after the initial signing date.

In Division II football, unlimited phone calls to you can be made during a contact period and once a week outside of a contact period.

Coaches may accept collect calls and use a toll-free (1–800) number to receive telephone calls from you (or your parents or legal guardians) at any time.

Enrolled students (including student-athletes) may not make recruiting telephone calls to you unless the calls are made as a part of an institution's regular admissions program directed at all prospective students. Enrolled students (including student-athletes) may receive telephone calls at your expense on or after July 1 after completion of your junior year.

You (or your family) may not receive any benefit, inducement or arrangement such as cash, clothing, cars, improper expenses, transportation, gifts or loans to encourage you to sign an institutional or conference letter of intent or to attend an NCAA school.

A college coach may contact you in person off the college campus but only on or after July 1 after completion of your junior year.

Any face-to-face meeting between a coach and you or your parents, during which any of you says more than "hello" is a contact. Furthermore, any face-to-face meeting that is prearranged, or occurs at your high school or at any competition or practice site is a contact, regardless of the conversation. These contacts are not permissible "bumps."

In all sports, coaches may contact you off the college campus three times. However, a coach may visit your high school (with your high-school principal's approval) only once a week during a contact period.

An evaluation is any off-campus activity used to assess your academic qualifications or athletics ability, including a visit to your high school (during which no contact occurs) or watching you practice or compete at any site.

In all sports, coaches may not evaluate you more than four times during the academic year. Competition on consecutive days within a tournament (and normally at the same site) or that involves a tier of a tournament (e.g., regional) counts as a single evaluation. Once you sign a National Letter of Intent, you may be evaluated an unlimited number of times by a college coach from the college with which you have signed.

In football and basketball only, there are specified periods when a coach may contact you off the college campus and/or attend your practices and games to evaluate your athletics ability.

1997–98 Contact Periods

Football—December 1, 1997, through March 9, 1998.

Men's Basketball—September 7 through October 14, 1997; March 1 through March 26, 1998; March 31 (noon) through April 6 (7 A.M.), 1998; April 8 (7 A.M.) through May 11, 1998.

Women's Basketball—September 7 through October 14, 1997; March 1 through April 6 (7 A.M.), 1998; April 8 (7 A.M.) through May 11, 1998.

1997–98 Evaluation Periods

Football—During any contact period; during November 1997 and May 1998; the period between the prospect's initial and final contests; during any high-school all-star game that occurs in the state where the college is located.

Men's Basketball—During any contact period; the period between the prospect's initial and final contests; June 15 through August 1; during any high-school all-star game that occurs in the state where the college is located.

Women's Basketball—During any contact period; the period between the prospect's initial and final contests; during any sanctioned AAU competition between May 18 and June 14; June 15 through August 1; during any high-school all-star game that occurs in the state where the college is located.

[Note: There is a "dead" period (coaches may not contact or evaluate you on or off the college campus) in all sports 48 hours before 7 A.M. on the initial signing date for the National Letter of Intent.]

With the permission of your high school's director of athletics, you may try out for a college team before enrollment. The tryout must occur after your high-school eligibility is completed and may include tests to evaluate your strength, speed, agility and sports skills. Except in football, ice hockey, lacrosse, soccer and wrestling, the tryout may include competition.

You can visit a college campus any time at your expense. On such a visit, you may receive three complimentary admissions to a game on that campus, a tour of off-campus practice and competition sites in your sport and other facilities within 30 miles of the campus, and a meal for you and your parents or guardians in the college's on-campus student dining facilities.

Official Visits

During your senior year, you can have one expense-paid (official) visit to a particular campus. You may receive no more than a total of five such visits. This restriction applies even if you are being recruited in more than one sport. A college may not give you an official visit unless you have provided it with a PSAT, ACT or SAT score from a test taken on a national testing date under national testing conditions.

During your official visit (which may not exceed 48 hours), you may receive round-trip transportation between your home (or high school) and the campus, and you (and your parents) may receive meals, lodging and complimentary admissions to campus athletics events. In addition, a student host may help you (and your family) become acquainted with campus life. The host may spend $30 per day to cover costs of entertaining you (and your parents, legal guardians or spouse); however, the money cannot be used to purchase college souvenirs such as T-shirts or other college mementos.

Printed Materials

A Division II college recruiting you may provide to you only the following printed materials on or after September 1 at the beginning of your junior year:

- Official academic, admissions and student-services publications or videotapes published by the college

- General correspondence, including letters and college note cards

- Newspaper clippings, provided they are not assembled in any form of a scrapbook

- A media guide or recruiting brochure (but not both) in each sport

- Game programs (a college may only give you a program on an official or unofficial visit; colleges may not mail you a program)

- Any preenrollment information about orientation, conditioning, academics, and (or) practice activities, as long as you have signed a National Letter of Intent or have been accepted for enrollment by a member college

- One student-athlete handbook. (A college may only give you a handbook on an official or unofficial visit. A college may not mail it to you.)

- One wallet-size playing schedule card in each sport.

In addition, a Division II college may show you a highlight film/ videotape, but may not send it to you or leave it with you or your coach.

Finally, a Division II college also may provide you with a questionnaire, camp brochure and educational information published by the NCAA (such as this guide) at any time.

Division III

In addition to general recruiting regulations, you (or your family) may not receive any benefit, inducement or arrangement such as cash, clothing, cars, improper expenses, transportation, gifts or loans to encourage you to attend any NCAA school.

An athletics department staff member, alumni or representative of a college's athletics interests (boosters or representatives) may contact you in person off the college campus after your junior year of high school. There is no limit on the number of contacts or the period when they may occur. You may not try out for a Division III college's athletics team. A tryout is any physical activity (e.g., practice session or test) conducted by or arranged on behalf of a college at which you display your ability.

You can visit a college campus any time at your own expense. On such a visit, you may receive three complimentary admissions to a game on that campus; a tour of off-campus practice and competition sites in your sport and other college facilities within 30 miles of the campus; a meal in the college's on-campus student dining facilities; and housing, if it is available to all visiting prospective students.

Official Visits

During your senior year, you can make one expense-paid (official) visit to a particular campus; however, there is no limit on the number of campuses that you may visit if you initially enroll in a Division III college.

During your official visit (which may not exceed 48 hours), you may receive round-trip transportation between your home (or high school) and the campus, and you (and your parents) may receive meals, lodging and complimentary admissions to campus athletics events. All meals provided to you (and/or your parents) on an official visit must occur in an on-campus dining facility that the college's students normally use. If dining facilities are closed, the college is permitted to take you off-campus for meals. In addition, a student host may help you (and your family) become acquainted with campus life. The host may spend $20 per day to cover all costs of entertaining you (and your parents, legal guardians or spouse); however, the money can't be used to purchase college souvenirs such as T-shirts or other college mementos.

Finally, a Division III college is permitted to provide you and your high-school and/or two-year college coach any official academic, admissions, athletics and student-services publications published by the college and other general information available to all students.

National Letter of Intent

The National Letter of Intent is administered by the Collegiate Commissioners Association, not the NCAA. There are restrictions on signing

1997–98 National Letter of Intent Signing Dates (Approved by Collegiate Commissioners Association)		
Sport	**Initial Date**	**Final Date**
Basketball (Early Period)	Nov. 12, 1997	Nov. 19, 1997
Basketball (Late Period)	April 8, 1998	May 15, 1998
Football (Midyear JC transfer)	Dec. 17, 1997	Jan. 15, 1998
Football (Regular)	Feb. 4, 1998	April 1, 1998
Women's Volleyball, Field Hockey, Soccer, Men's Water Polo	Feb. 4, 1998	Aug. 1, 1998
All Other Sports (Early Period)	Nov. 12, 1997	Nov. 19, 1997
All Other Sports (Late Period)	April 8, 1998	Aug. 1, 1998

Note: These dates are subject to change.

a National Letter of Intent that may affect your eligibility. These restrictions are contained in the letter of intent. Read it carefully. If you have questions about the National Letter of Intent signing dates or restrictions about signing, contact the conference office of the college you are interested in attending. Please note that some conferences don't subscribe to the National Letter of Intent program.

Remember, do not sign any institutional or conference letter of intent (or financial aid agreement) before the National Letter of Intent signing date.

Professionalism

Don't lose your college eligibility by becoming a professional.

You are a "professional" if you:

● Are paid (in any form) or accept the promise of pay for playing in an athletics contest

● Sign a contract or verbally commit with an agent or a professional sports organization

● Ask that your name be placed on a draft list [Note: In basketball, once you become a student-athlete at an NCAA school, you may enter a professional league's draft one time without jeopardizing your eligibility provided you are not drafted by any team in that league and you declare your intention in writing to return to college within 30 days after the draft]

● Use your athletics skill for pay in any form (for example, TV commercials, demonstrations)

● Play on a professional athletics team, or

● Participate on any amateur sports team and receive any salary, incentive payment, award, gratuity, educational expenses or expense allowances (other than playing apparel, equipment and actual and necessary travel, and room and board expenses).

Before enrolling in college, you may:

● Try out (practice with but not participate against outside competition) with a professional sports team at your expense

- Receive actual and necessary expenses from any professional sports organizations for one visit per professional organization not in excess of 48 hours, and

- Receive a fee for teaching a lesson in a particular sport

Agents

During high school, you might be contacted by a player agent. A player agent may want to represent you in contract negotiations or for commercial endorsements if you show the potential to be a professional athlete. Agents may contact you during your high-school years to gain an advantage over other individuals who may wish to represent you when your college eligibility expires. Many times, these individuals will not represent themselves as agents, but rather as someone interested in your overall welfare and athletics career. These individuals also may try to give gifts or benefits to you and your family.

NCAA rules don't prohibit meetings or discussions with an agent. However, you jeopardize your college eligibility in a sport if you agree (orally or in writing) to be represented by an agent while in high school or college, regardless of whether the agreement becomes effective immediately or after your last season of college eligibility. Also, receiving any benefits or gifts by you, your family or friends from a player agent would jeopardize your college eligibility.

If an individual contacts you about marketing your athletics ability, please be careful. If you have concerns about a player agent, contact your high-school coach, director of athletics or the NCAA national office for assistance.

Drug Testing

If you attend an NCAA school, you will be subject to regulations prohibiting drug use. Each academic year in Divisions I and II sports in which the NCAA conducts year-round drug testing (currently Divisions I and II football and track and field), you must sign a drug-testing consent form when you report for practice or before the Monday of your college's fourth week of classes, whichever occurs earlier. In all other Divisions I and II sports and in Division III each academic year, you must sign a drug-testing consent form before you compete. Drug testing occurs randomly on a year-round basis in Divisions I and II football and track and field. Drug testing also is conducted at NCAA championships and football bowl games. If you test positive, you will lose a season of competition in all sports if the season of competition has not yet started. If the season of competition has started, you will lose one full season of competition in all sports (i.e., remaining contests in the current season and contests in the following season up to the time that you were declared ineligible during the previous year). In addition, many colleges have their own drug-use policies that may affect your participation.

Further, the use of tobacco products is prohibited for coaches, game officials and student-athletes in all sports during practice and competition. A student-athlete who uses tobacco products during practice or competition is automatically disqualified for the remainder of that practice or game.

Graduation Rates

To help you in selecting a college, the NCAA national office annually publishes Divisions I, II and III admissions and graduation-rate information. To make the information easy to get, the Division I or II college recruiting you must provide its graduation-rate information to you, as well your parents, at the earlier of the following opportunities: (1) upon request by you or your parents, or (2) after the school's first arranged in-person meeting with you (or your parents) but not later than the day before you sign a National Letter of Intent or an offer of admission and/or financial aid.

In addition, the NCAA national office sends graduation-rate information annually to your high school.

What to Ask

The following questions and information were developed by the NCAA Student-Athlete Advisory Committee. The committee urges prospective student-athletes to ask these types of questions during their recruitment.

Athletics

Q *What positions will I play on your team?*

● It's not always obvious.

● Most coaches want to be flexible so that you are not disappointed.

Q *Describe the other players competing at the same position.*

● If there is a former high-school all-American at that position, you may want to take that into consideration.

● This will give you clues as to what year you might be a starter.

Q *Can I "redshirt" my first year?*

● Find out how common it is to redshirt and how that will affect graduation.

● Does the school redshirt you if you are injured?

Q *What are the physical requirements each year?*

● Philosophies of strength and conditioning vary by institution.

● You may be required to maintain a certain weight.

Q *How would you best describe your coaching style?*

● Every coach has a particular style that involves different motivational techniques and discipline.

● You need to know if a coach's teaching style does not match your learning style.

Q *What is the game plan?*

● For team sports, find out what kind of offense and defense is employed.

● For individual sports, find out how you are seeded and how to qualify for conference and national championships.

Q *When does the head coach's contract end?*

● Don't make any assumptions about how long a coach will be at a school.

● If the coach is losing and the contract ends in two years, you may have a new coach.

Q *Describe the preferred, invited and uninvited walk-on situation. How many make it, compete and earn a scholarship?*

● Different teams treat walk-ons differently.

Academics

Q *How good is the department in my major?*

● Smaller colleges can have very highly rated departments.

● A team's reputation is only one variable to consider.

Q *What percentage of players on scholarship graduate in four years?*

● This will tell you about the quality of their commitment to academics.

● The team's grade-point average also is a good indicator of the coach's commitment to academics.

College Life

Q *Describe the typical class size.*

● At larger schools, classes are likely to be larger and taught by teaching assistants.

● Average class size is important to the amount of attention you receive.

Q *Describe in detail your academic support program. For example: Study-hall requirements, tutor availability, staff, class load, faculty cooperation.*

● This is imperative for marginal students.

● Find a college that will take the 3.000 students and help them get a 3.500 GPA.

Q *Describe the typical day for a student-athlete.*

● This will give you a good indication of how much time is spent in class, practice, studying and traveling.

● It also will give you a good indication of what coaches expect.

Q *What are the residence halls like?*

● Make sure you would feel comfortable in study areas, community bathrooms and laundry facilities.

● Number of students in a room and coed dorms are other variables to consider.

Q *Will I be required to live on campus throughout my athletics participation?*

● If the answer is yes, ask whether there are exceptions.

● Apartment living may be better than dorm living.

Financial Aid

Q *How much financial aid is available for summer school?*

● There is no guarantee. Get a firm commitment.

● You may need to lighten your normal load and go to summer school in order to graduate in four years. You can take graduate courses and maintain your eligibility.

Q *What are the details of financial aid at your institution?*

● What does my scholarship cover?

● What can I receive in addition to the scholarship and how do I get more aid?

Q *How long does my scholarship last?*

● Most people think a "full ride" is good for four years.

● Financial aid is available on a one-year renewable basis.

Q *If I'm injured, what happens to my financial aid?*

● A grant-in-aid is not guaranteed past a one-year period even for injuries.

● It is important to know if a school has a commitment to assist student-athletes for more than a year after they have been injured.

Q *What are my opportunities for employment while I'm a student?*

● Find out if you can be employed in-season, out-of-season or during vacation periods.

● NCAA rules prohibit you from earning more than the cost of attendance during the academic year.

Additional Comments

Scouting Services

● During high school, you might be contacted by a scouting service. NCAA rules prohibit scouting services from receiving payment based on the amount of your college scholarship. The NCAA does not sanction or endorse any scouting service. Therefore, attempt to determine whether the scouting service meets NCAA requirements.

All-Star Contests

● After your high-school eligibility is completed and before graduation, you can participate in two high-school all-star football or basketball contests in each sport.

Transfer Students

● If you transfer from a two-year or four-year college to an NCAA school, you must satisfy certain requirements before being eligible to participate in athletics at that college. Call the NCAA office if you have questions about transfer requirements. You can order free of charge the NCAA Student-Athlete Transfer Guide by calling 800-638-3731.

Student-Athlete Statement

● Each academic year, you must sign a statement about your eligibility, recruitment, financial aid and amateur status under NCAA rules. Don't jeopardize your eligibility by violating NCAA rules.

Conference Regulations

● Conferences may have additional regulations about recruiting, eligibility and financial aid. Ask your recruiter or the conference office about these rules.

Reporting Rule Violations

● If you think you have been improperly or unfairly recruited, notify the conference office or the NCAA.

● Knowingly furnishing the NCAA or your college false or misleading information about your involvement or knowledge of a rules violation will make you ineligible.

NCAA eligibility rules are sometimes complex as they apply to certain students. This guide should not be relied upon exclusively. Contact the NCAA office or appropriate conference office for proper interpretations in specific cases. Your inquiries should be addressed to the NCAA legislative services staff at 6201 College Boulevard, Overland Park, Kansas 66211-2422.

Sport-by-Sport Breakdown

Below is a list of sports played at the collegiate level with the number of schools that play that sport. These numbers are to give you a basic idea of your chances of receiving either a scholarship or a chance to play your sport in college.

The numbers refer to the year 1996. Keep in mind that due to budget cuts, Title IX gender equity fulfillment, and other factors, these numbers change constantly.

For more information about NCAA Divisions I, II, and III, NAIA, NSCAA, NCCAA, and junior colleges, see chapter 1.

Archery

Neither women's nor men's archery is an officially sponsored NCAA sport. The only scholarships available are at the junior colleges who compete.

Pro option: Not really, but money can made through exhibitions and small competitions.

Women

Division I: 2
Division II: 0
Division III: 1
NAIA: 0
NSCAA, NCCAA, unaffiliated: 1
Junior colleges: 3

Men

Division I: 2
Division II: 0
Division III: 1
NAIA: 0
NSCAA, NCCAA, unaffiliated: 0
Junior colleges: 2

Badminton

Women's badminton is not an officially sponsored NCAA sport. There are no scholarships available to play at the collegiate level.
Pro option: Nope.

Women

Division I: 0
Division II: 0
Division III: 0
NAIA: 0
NSCAA, NCCAA, unaffiliated: 2
Junior colleges: 0

Baseball

Men's baseball is played at almost 1,200 colleges and junior colleges so there is a lot of opportunity. Scholarships abound.
Pro option: Yes.

Men

Division I: 273
Division II: 166
Division III: 270
NAIA: 233
NSCAA, NCCAA, unaffiliated: 63
Junior colleges: 202

Basketball

Almost every school that fields a sports team fields a basketball team. If you can play, and you desperately want to play, there should be a place to play at some level. If you can play well, a scholarship or partial scholarship is very possible.
Pro option: Yes.

Women	Men
Division I: 292	Division I: 301
Division II: 218	Division II: 160
Division III: 321	Division III: 312
NAIA: 315	NAIA: 336
NSCAA, NCCAA, unaffiliated: 120	NSCAA, NCCAA, unaffiliated: 154
Junior colleges: 266	Junior colleges: 313

Bowling

Bowling is not an officially sponsored NCAA sport. There are, however, a few scholarships available at the Division I and junior college levels.

Pro option: Yes.

Women	Men
Division I: 2	Division I: 5
Division II: 4	Division II: 5
Division III: 2	Division III: 2
NAIA: 3	NAIA: 3
NSCAA, NCCAA, unaffiliated: 1	NSCAA, NCCAA, unaffiliated: 1
Junior colleges: 5	Junior colleges: 5

Cheerleading

Almost every school that has sports teams has cheerleaders, but the status of the squads, their instruction, and their facilities vary greatly. At a major Division I program, cheerleaders may be treated royally, but at a small school they might have to sell cookies to pay for their own uniforms. If you're interested in cheerleading in college, check if the school has a full-time or part-time coach and try to talk to one or two of the students on the squad to get a sense of what it's like.

Cheerleading in college can be demanding and time-consuming, so it's a good idea to know what the school's expectations are. Scholarships for cheerleading are virtually impossible to come by, but financial aid can occasionally be tied to other scholarship programs that the school might offer. Cheerleading is not an officially sponsored NCAA sport.

Pro option: No.

Crew

Basically the same for men as for women. The options are in the Northeast and the West at Division I, but schools around the country participate at the other levels. Most of the nation's top universities have excellent crew teams—this is a sport in which the Ivy League excels—but the Ivies don't offer sports scholarships and very few other schools offer money for rowers. There is, however, need-based aid. Crew is not an officially sponsored NCAA sport.

Pro option: Not really.

Women	Men
Division I: 39	Division I: 39
Division II: 11	Division II: 11
Division III: 20	Division III: 16
NAIA: 7	NAIA: 6
NSCAA, NCCAA, unaffiliated: 5	NSCAA, NCCAA, unaffiliated: 5
Junior colleges: 0	Junior colleges: 0

Cross-Country Running

You can run cross-country almost anywhere across the country and scholarships—often partial scholarships or tied to track scholarships—are available.

Pro option: Marathon running can be lucrative.

Women	Men
Division I: 277	Division I: 280
Division II: 165	Division II: 170
Division III: 258	Division III: 261
NAIA: 170	NAIA: 115
NSCAA, NCCAA, unaffiliated: 32	NSCAA, NCCAA, unaffiliated: 34
Junior colleges: 56	Junior colleges: 62

Equestrian Sports

Almost 60 colleges across the various divisions (more women than men) offer equestrian sports, but no scholarships are available at Divisions I, II, or III. Scholarships, however, are available at a few NAIA schools and small colleges and many of the junior colleges.

Pro option: Horse shows and the like. But it's expensive, too.

Women	Men
Division I: 4	Division I: 4
Division II: 5	Division II: 3
Division III: 19	Division III: 13
NAIA: 9	NAIA: 6
NSCAA, NCCAA, unaffiliated: 9	NSCAA, NCCAA, unaffiliated: 5
Junior colleges: 17	Junior colleges: 16

Fencing

Fencing is popular at many of the nation's elite colleges and universities across all divisions. Since a few schools in the so-called power conferences (Big 10, Big East, ACC) also have fencing teams, scholarships are available, but extremely difficult to come by. You better be good and you better be smart.

Pro option: Not yet.

Women	Men
Division I: 23	Division I: 23
Division II: 4	Division II: 4
Division III: 17	Division III: 20
NAIA: 3	NAIA: 3
NSCAA, NCCAA, unaffiliated: 4	NSCAA, NCCAA, unaffiliated: 5
Junior colleges: 1	Junior colleges: 1

Field Hockey

Primarily a sport played in the northeastern United States, there are a few field hockey teams across the country and scholarships are available.
Pro option: Not really.

Women

Division I: 64
Division II: 22
Division III: 117
NAIA: 8
NSCAA, NCCAA, unaffiliated: 10
Junior colleges: 5

Football

With basketball, the key revenue-producing sport in college. More than 700 schools play football and there are a lot of players on each football team. Scholarships are most definitely available.
Pro option: Yes.

Men

Division I-A: 105
Division I-AA: 116

Division II: 126
Division III: 209
NAIA: 120
NSCAA, NCCAA, unaffiliated: 13
Junior colleges: 54

Golf

Golf is played everywhere but is especially popular in the Southeast
and the Southwest. Scholarships are available.
  Pro option: Yes.

Women

Division I: 131
Division II: 22
Division III: 53
NAIA: 56
NSCAA, NCCAA, unaffiliated: 19
Junior colleges: 47

Men

Division I: 268
Division II: 135
Division III: 209
NAIA: 181
NSCAA, NCCAA, unaffiliated: 46
Junior colleges: 151

Gymnastics

More women than men's teams and they're spread across the country. Scholarships are available.
  Pro option: Not really, but a top gymnast can make money from
endorsements and exhibitions. Women are generally past the world-
class stage by the time they reach college. Men can be stars in and after college.

Women

Division I: 65
Division II: 11
Division III: 14
NAIA: 0

Men

Division I: 32
Division II: 2
Division III: 2
NAIA: 1

NSCAA, NCCAA, unaffiliated: 3   NSCAA, NCCAA, unaffiliated: 3
Junior colleges: 0   Junior colleges: 0

Ice Hockey

Women's hockey is not an officially sponsored NCAA sport, but colleges in the northeastern United States (including six of the eight Ivy schools) have women's hockey teams. Men's hockey is an officially sponsored NCAA sport and scholarships are available throughout the Northeast and the Midwest.
Pro option: Yes for men.

Women

Division I: 10
Division II: 0
Division III: 5
NAIA: 0
NSCAA, NCCAA, unaffiliated: 3
Junior colleges: 1

Men

Division I: 51
Division II: 16
Division III: 67
NAIA: 3
NSCAA, NCCAA, unaffiliated: 4
Junior colleges: 2

Lacrosse

Like field hockey, lacrosse is prominent in the Northeast. But unlike field hockey, it's also played by men. Scholarships are available.
Pro option: Yes, for men in indoor lacrosse.

Women

Division I: 36
Division II: 13
Division III: 82
NAIA: 2
NSCAA, NCCAA, unaffiliated: 3
Junior colleges: 1

Men

Division I: 57
Division II: 26
Division III: 95
NAIA: 11
NSCAA, NCCAA, unaffiliated: 4
Junior colleges: 6

Riflery

Schools around the country field riflery teams, but not many of them. Scholarships are available.

Pro option: A skilled marksman can make a living any of a number of ways.

Women

Division I: 17
Division II: 3
Division III: 7
NAIA: 3
NSCAA, NCCAA, unaffiliated: 1
Junior colleges: 0

Men

Division I: 27
Division II: 4
Division III: 10
NAIA: 3
NSCAA, NCCAA, unaffiliated: 1
Junior colleges: 4

Rugby

Not an officially recognized NCAA sport. No scholarships are available.

Pro option: Not in the United States.

Men

Division I: 4
Division II: 2
Division III: 12
NAIA: 3
NSCAA, NCCAA, unaffiliated: 5
Junior colleges: 0

Sailing

Not an officially recognized NCAA sport. No scholarships are available.

Pro option: It takes money to make money.

Women	Men
Division I: 10	Division I: 13
Division II: 2	Division II: 3
Division III: 13	Division III: 14
NAIA: 2	NAIA: 2
NSCAA, NCCAA, unaffiliated: 4	NSCAA, NCCAA, unaffiliated: 4
Junior colleges: 1	Junior colleges: 1

Skiing (Cross-Country)

Another sport found primarily in the Northeast. A few scholarships are available.
Pro option: Not in the United States.

Women	Men
Division I: 8	Division I: 9
Division II: 6	Division II: 6
Division III: 10	Division III: 10
NAIA: 7	NAIA: 7
NSCAA, NCCAA, unaffiliated: 3	NSCAA, NCCAA, unaffiliated: 3
Junior colleges: 2	Junior colleges: 2

Skiing (Downhill)

As might be expected, downhill skiing teams can be found at schools near mountains and snow. Scholarships are available.
Pro option: Yes, for a very few.

Women	Men
Division I: 11	Division I: 11
Division II: 5	Division II: 5
Division III: 12	Division III: 12
NAIA: 9	NAIA: 10
NSCAA, NCCAA, unaffiliated: 3	NSCAA, NCCAA, unaffiliated: 3
Junior colleges: 5	Junior colleges: 5

Soccer

Men can play soccer almost anywhere and opportunities are growing for women. Scholarships are available.

Pro option: Yes for men, especially internationally. Not as strong a yes for women. Give it a few years.

Women

Division I: 109
Division II: 74
Division III: 223
NAIA: 117
NSCAA, NCCAA, unaffiliated: 26
Junior colleges: 31

Men

Division I: 189
Division II: 120
Division III: 284
NAIA: 222
NSCAA, NCCAA, unaffiliated: 96
Junior colleges: 76

Softball

Women's softball is played across the country and scholarships are available. Men's softball is not an officially sponsored NCAA sport, but a handful of scholarships are available.

Pro option: There are leagues for women, especially semipro. Men can play in the park or on exhibition teams.

Women

Division I: 192
Division II: 159
Division III: 237
NAIA: 147
NSCAA, NCCAA, unaffiliated: 37
Junior colleges: 144

Men

Division I: 1
Division II: 2
Division III: 5
NAIA: 4
NSCAA, NCCAA, unaffiliated: 1
Junior colleges: 4

Squash

Not an officially recognized NCAA sport. No scholarships are available.
Pro option: Sort of, but if you play squash you probably don't need the money.

Women	Men
Division I: 7	Division I: 9
Division II: 2	Division II: 1
Division III: 16	Division III: 18
NAIA: 0	NAIA: 1
NSCAA, NCCAA, unaffiliated: 0	NSCAA, NCCAA, unaffiliated: 0
Junior colleges: 1	Junior colleges: 0

Swimming and Diving

Not nearly as many schools as you might expect have swimming programs, so spots are highly competitive. Scholarships are available.
Pro option: Not really. Kind of surprising.

Women	Men
Division I: 162	Division I: 157
Division II: 55	Division II: 51
Division III: 180	Division III: 68
NAIA: 27	NAIA: 30
NSCAA, NCCAA, unaffiliated: 6	NSCAA, NCCAA, unaffiliated: 4
Junior colleges: 9	Junior colleges: 9

Tennis

Most schools field tennis teams, but a lot of people play tennis so you still have to be good. Scholarships are available.
Pro option: Yes.

Women

Division I: 280
Division II: 172
Division III: 291
NAIA: 199
NSCAA, NCCAA, unaffiliated: 53
Junior colleges: 96

Men

Division I: 276
Division II: 155
Division III: 279
NAIA: 195
NSCAA, NCCAA, unaffiliated: 47
Junior colleges: 109

Track and Field

Track is a very popular college sport at all levels and scholarships are available.
Pro option: Yes.

Women

Division I: 246
Division II: 116
Division III: 209
NAIA: 125
NSCAA, NCCAA, unaffiliated: 24
Junior colleges: 51

Men

Division I: 244
Division II: 130
Division III: 208
NAIA: 136
NSCAA, NCCAA, unaffiliated: 24
Junior colleges: 69

Volleyball

Played almost everywhere. Teams from the West are particularly strong. Scholarships are available.
Pro option: Yes, especially on the beach.

Women

Division I: 271
Division II: 201
Division III: 297
NAIA: 275

Men

Division I: 31
Division II: 16
Division III: 28
NAIA: 16

NSCAA, NCCAA, unaffiliated: 129 NSCAA, NCCAA, unaffiliated: 19
Junior colleges: 200 Junior colleges: 5

Water Polo

Water polo is not (yet) an officially sponsored sport for women. For men, scholarships are available.
Pro option: Not in the United States.

Women

Division I: 2
Division II: 1
Division III: 6
NAIA: 0
NSCAA, NCCAA, unaffiliated: 0
Junior colleges: 0

Men

Division I: 25
Division II: 6
Division III: 15
NAIA: 0
NSCAA, NCCAA, unaffiliated: 2
Junior colleges: 0

Wrestling

Popular across the country, especially in the Northeast and the Midwest. Scholarships are available.
Pro option: Let's not talk about it.

Men

Division I: 108
Division II: 46
Division III: 102
NAIA: 26
NSCAA, NCCAA, unaffiliated: 8
Junior colleges: 30

Index

About the Authors

Basketball player and coach **Perry Bromwell** attended Don Bosco Tech in Boston and Avon Old Farms in Connecticut. As a freshman at Manhattan College, Bromwell was chosen Metro Conference Basketball Rookie of the Year (1982–83). After transferring to the University of Pennsylvania, Bromwell was a three-time All-Ivy performer—and Ivy Player of the Year in 1987—twice leading the Quakers to the NCAA basketball tournament. Bromwell graduated from Penn in 1987 with a degree in communications and was a sixth-round draft choice of the NBA New Jersey Nets. His postcollege basketball career includes one season with the New Jersey Jammers of the USBL in 1987 and stints as a player and/or coach with Manchester United, London Docklands, and the University of Nottingham in England; the CBA's Quad City Thunder; and Crispa of the Philippine Basketball League. He has also worked as a teacher in the Philadelphia public schools and for the past two seasons has been a player-coach for a professional team in Norway.

Howard Gensler has worked as an editor at the *Philadelphia Daily News* and at *TV Guide* magazine and has written for *TV Guide, Premiere, PhillySport, College Sports, Sports Travel,* the *Philadelphia Inquirer, BusinessTraveler, Yahoo! Internet Life,* and *TV Guide Online.* He is also the coauthor of the books *Pride of the Palestra: 90 Years of Pennsylvania Basketball* and *Managing for Quality and Survival.* He lives in Philadelphia.